Modelling the [...]de

A GUIDE FOR RAILWAY MODELLERS

Modelling the Lineside

A GUIDE FOR RAILWAY MODELLERS

RICHARD BARDSLEY

THE CROWOOD PRESS

First published in 2016 by
The Crowood Press Ltd
Ramsbury, Marlborough
Wiltshire SN8 2HR

www.crowood.com

British Library Cataloguing-in-Publication Data
A catalogue record for this book is available from the British Library.

ISBN 978 1 78500 139 0

ACKNOWLEDGEMENTS
This book is dedicated to my mother Margaret Bardsley, who passed away while it was being
written; she was proud of my first three books and would have loved this one just as much. I am
extremely grateful to my wife Sharon Bardsley for her continued support while also looking
after our little boy, Samuel. As with each book I have written, thanks go to my father Stuart
Bardsley for his keen proofing skills, but, in addition, he has constructed many of the model kits
shown in this book, as well as going out and about for prototype photographs. My train buddy
Colin Whalley was as generous as ever in lending me various models to photograph. For
permission to use their superb photos, I thank Steve Flint and Craig Tiley of *Railway Modeller*. For
letting me photograph their 'Glazebrook' layout, I once again thank my friends at the Warrington
Model Railway Club.

Typeset and designed by D & N Publishing, Baydon, Wiltshire

Printed and bound in India by Replika Press Pvt Ltd

CONTENTS

INTRODUCTION

One of the joys of being a railway enthusiast is to be able to turn up at the side of a railway line and just watch the trains go by. The more important the line, such as a main line or major route, then the more trains you will see. Being 'lineside' is great fun, whether you are a serious 'trainspotter', or just a casual enthusiast. Who would not want to recreate this spectacle in model form?

With your very own model railway layout you can go 'linesiding' whenever you want. It is easy to think that a railway line is just track, but there is more to it than meets the eye. There may be signals and a signal box, the boundary fence, warning signs, a platelayers' hut, a track gang – any or all of these things may be visible in a short stretch of railway line. As modellers, we can incorporate these features to provide an authentic and detailed backdrop for the trains themselves.

Real trains rarely use a railway line with the high frequency that model ones do. So if you spend a little bit of time at a real lineside location, you will doubtless have time between the trains. You could read a good book, but, instead, use the time to study the place

and all the little details that can be found there. It is surprising what you will start to notice once you pay attention to these details. Then you can think about incorporating these things into your model railway.

Many things like signals and level crossings can be found at stations, though they may also be found in the middle of nowhere at a point between two stations. So stations are a good place for research, taking away the station itself and using the remaining features to model a stretch of the line.

Signalling is one of the most common features to be found by the lineside, since signals are not just used to start and stop trains at stations. The block working system means that signals (and signal boxes) could be found in what are often quite isolated places. Junctions are not necessarily found at stations, therefore the signals for these locations can be seen where you might not expect to find them.

There are many reasons to cross the railway line, so bridges, level crossings and underpasses can be found all along the lineside. Conversely, there are many places where the railway company does not want people to

While today's Rainford Junction is but a shadow of its former self, this view shows a wealth of detail that can be included in a lineside scene. Besides the obvious features such as the signal box and the signals themselves, there are many important details. These include the signs (both speed signs and warning signs for personnel), the unguarded 'barrow' crossing for the signalman, streetlamps for night-time, a traffic cone and even a short length of discarded rail.

cross the line; to prevent trespass there are all sorts of styles of boundary fencing and walling.

Dotted along the lineside there were, and in some cases still are, various buildings in support of the operation of the railway. Most obviously there are signal boxes and equally common were the platelayers' huts. Sometimes a level crossing in an isolated place would have had a crossing keeper's cottage.

Some of the details are smaller, such as gradient signs, mileposts and speed signs. Ballast bins can be seen by platelayers' huts, or just on their own along the lineside. Sadly, many places attract rubbish, from small items to big ones; it is a small detail, but if you really want to be authentic about modelling a time and a place then you need to include it.

Railway lines consist of track and like the rolling stock that uses it, track needs regular maintenance and eventually renewal. An interesting cameo scene can be created at the lineside by modelling the men, materials and equipment that are needed to keep the track well maintained and safe.

While railways have always run on track, the lineside details can set the period and scene instantly. There is a broad distinction between the steam period and the modernization era. The former would have been characterized by such things as telegraph poles, platelayers' huts (and platelayers) and semaphore signals. The modern railway era is one of concrete trunking, mobile track gangs in vans and colour light signals.

Some things do timelessly cross these two broad eras. There are still some signal boxes and semaphore signals in use today, though this small minority is declining quickly. While modernity is not to be found in a period setting, the old can often be discovered alongside the new. It may be out of use, but often it is still there, for example as a boarded-up signal box or a ruined platelayers' hut.

A seemingly ordinary lineside scene can actually contain a lot of detail, as this view of the Warrington Model Railway Club's N-gauge layout 'Glazebrook' demonstrates. In the foreground, there is wire-in-post fencing, while at the top of the embankment is a tall vertical planked fence. There is an elevated signal box (giving clearance to see over the bridge), as well as signals to control the junction that begins bottom left. Finally, aside from the locomotive, the steam era is much in evidence by virtue of the telegraph poles.

Fortunately for railway modellers, much of the detail that brings a lineside scene to life is readily available from the model railway manufacturers. Some of it is available ready to plant; all you have to do is take it out of the box and install it on your layout. Other items are available as good-quality kits, so if you enjoy making things there is the added bonus of putting them together. In some cases, what you need may not be available ready-made or as a kit, but scratch-building is not as difficult as it may seem.

Lineside details may be found in isolation, but they can also be found in logical groups. A signal might be on its own, or it might be beside a signal box. The boundary will be defined by a fence or wall, and in the steam era there would have been telegraph poles. It is up to you how much or how little detail you incorporate on to your layout; combining related details at one point can provide an interesting cameo scene that will hold your attention and interest, even when trains are not running.

To the casual observer, the lineside may just seem to be all track and ballast. In many places, this is certainly not the case and there is a wealth of detail to be included to build a model railway that looks just like the real thing. One of the greatest modelling challenges is often the attempt to model the mundane, the everyday and the commonplace. Much of the lineside falls into this category. Fortunately, it is simple to achieve. With a great-looking model railway lineside, you can just sit back and watch the trains go by. You will think that you really are there, back by the lineside where you spent many happy hours all that time ago.

Modelling the lineside can take you back to another place and time. 'Tunley Marsh' is a small N-gauge layout with a single track that is set in the 1930s. In the short space between the station and fiddle yard can be seen some classic lineside elements: a signal box; platelayers' hut; signal; and lineside fencing.

CHAPTER ONE

LINESIDE LAYOUTS

It might seem an odd statement, but the first thing is to understand what actually constitutes the lineside. There is an assumption that every layout needs to have a station, but this is not true. If you want to focus on just the railway line and therefore the lineside, then why not? A layout can be specifically designed with these things in mind so that the finished model delivers exactly what you want. Principally, the design of such a layout will seek to maximize the amount of visible railway line so that long trains can been seen in their natural environment, whether that's a rural or urban setting.

DEFINING THE LINESIDE

At the highest level, a railway is a network of connecting lines that joins cities and major towns. Each

Most layouts include at least one station, although it is not what you would think of as the lineside since the station is an entity in itself. It might contain elements of the lineside, such as the boundary fence that can be seen in this view of N-gauge layout 'Tunley Marsh', but most of the other features are specialist station infrastructure such as platforms and a goods yard.

line that makes such a connection will travel through various places en route, be they large or small. There is a tendency to think of railways in terms of stations; the destinations matter more than the journey. Yet stations account for a tiny fraction of the whole route mileage. The vast majority of a railway line exists between the places that it serves.

The lineside can therefore be found between the stations and yards that form the destinations for railway journeys. Of course, you can stand by the railway line at a station, but here there is specialist infrastructure in the form of platforms to enable you to stand safely right next to the track and to interface with a passenger train in order to make your journey. Even non-stopping trains will slow for a station, so if you want full steam ahead, you will need to model the railway as it is away from the stations.

Outside of the station environment, the railway line has a boundary, the limit of the land that the railway owns, and of the infrastructure that it is responsible for and maintains. Railway land is privately owned, so trespass is discouraged, not least for the safety of passing ramblers and sheep. In order to avoid any dangerous trespass, railways have provided the means to cross the railway safely, such as bridges and level crossings.

As a train enthusiast, you stand at the lineside, but you are really standing on the very edge of the railway itself and at the limit of where you are allowed to tread. The lineside extends from the edge of the rails themselves to the boundary fence that is the limit of the railway's responsibility. That narrow strip of land that wends its way across the country is both the railway and the lineside at the same time.

As DMU 175 005 passes through Winwick Junction near Warrington on 11 October 2010, the focus of attention for the railway enthusiast is probably on the train rather than the lineside. Yet there is a wealth of detail to be observed beside the towering posts for the overhead power lines. On the near side of the line there is wire-in-post fencing (with mesh to keep the farmer's livestock off the railway), while on the far side is modern steel palisade fencing. There are four relay cabinets in differing shades of grey (and rust), small warning signs for trackworkers and larger speed signs for drivers.

The vast majority of the railway and the lineside is plain, with perhaps just the boundary fence to be modelled. Yet in certain places there are interesting features that are just as challenging to model realistically as a station is. There are small details like a platelayers' hut tucked away at the side, all the way up to lengthy water troughs with their attendant water towers.

The railway modeller can take as much care over modelling these plain out-of-the-way locations as he would modelling a station. The lineside is perhaps just a backdrop for the trains, but if you get it wrong, it will not look the part and will detract from the aim of presenting the trains in a realistic setting.

DOES A LAYOUT NEED A STATION?

There is a perceived wisdom that every model railway layout should have at least one station. It is true that a station provides plenty of operational possibilities. You can stop and start trains, shunt the goods yard and reverse trains to send them back from whence they came. There is a feeling that stations are what trains are all about; however, stations are but a tiny fraction of the whole railway network.

Unless you possess a railway room that is as big as a barn, it will be necessary to trade off one element of a model railway for another. The biggest problem for the modeller is that stations tend to take up a lot of room. We would all like a bigger model railway, but ultimately only so much can be fitted into the available space. This usually means making choices, a sacrifice here for a gain there. If a station dominates the layout, there is virtually no room to model the railway beyond the station limits. For many layouts, particularly terminus-type layouts, the station ends where the fiddle yard begins.

Even where space allows for some modelling of the railway line beyond the station, there may not be enough to hold an entire train. If you have a short stretch of line with long trains, the train may be entering the fiddle yard while the last coach is still clearing the platform. In such cases, there is no sense of

the train being out on the open line between stations. Additionally, an accelerating train may not even be at full line speed by the time it reaches the fiddle yard.

Being at the lineside is all about watching the trains pass by – so do you need a station at all? If you see the layout as a stage on which to display a collection of trains in an authentic surrounding, then a station may just get in the way. In recent years, a number of exhibition layouts have adopted the idea that you do not actually need to model a station on a layout. These layouts prove that modelling an open stretch of main line between stations is just as exciting. It allows for scale-length trains that can be seen running at full speed.

It is not just about using the space for a station, or for something else. There is a whole change of mindset brought about by abandoning the station altogether. It says that the focus of the model railway is going to be totally different, but, above all, it is going to be all about the trains. Accurately modelling the lineside will support this objective, but it will only work if the lineside is realistic and natural.

MAXIMIZING THE LENGTH OF THE RUN

Railways are long and thin. Even if Britain had adopted Brunel's broad gauge and six tracks on each route, the width that they take up would be minuscule compared to their overall length. This ratio of width to length presents railway modellers with a problem – rarely is there enough space available for a 'decent run'. Depth is less of a problem since most baseboards will be deep enough for the typical double-track main line.

The real restriction is that there is often not enough length. If you are modelling a branch line, then you will model trains that are quite short, just a pair of coaches in most cases. Modelling a main line means the desire to model main line trains. An express train can easily be twelve coaches long and some freight trains can be even longer. Unless you have a very large space, if you want to model just trains in the landscape, the first step is to omit any stations. The approach to the station at each end and then the length of the platforms take up a considerable amount of space. Often, a goods yard was beyond the platforms rather than behind them, which increases the length still further (a plan that suits a baseboard that is not very wide). The tendency to put the station in the middle of the scenic part of the layout means that you usually have two very short sections of lineside on either side of the station.

Do not be too concerned about needing to have curves rather than straight track. While railway engineers like to build their lines as straight as possible, you would be surprised how much the lines actually snake through the landscape as they follow the contours of valleys and hills. A driver's eye view is often quite illuminating in this respect. In fact, completely straight tracks in model form can serve to emphasize the narrow nature of a baseboard, so a little curvature from one side to another can look more pleasing even on the straight baseboards.

Curves become a concern for model railways at the corners of a room. Here they must turn through at least 90 degrees and sharp radii are often required. These can look unrealistic so they are often hidden in a tunnel.

Equally important is to have some kind of fiddle yard. The fiddle yard represents the rest of the railway network and the places where the trains on your layout are coming from and going to. You will need a

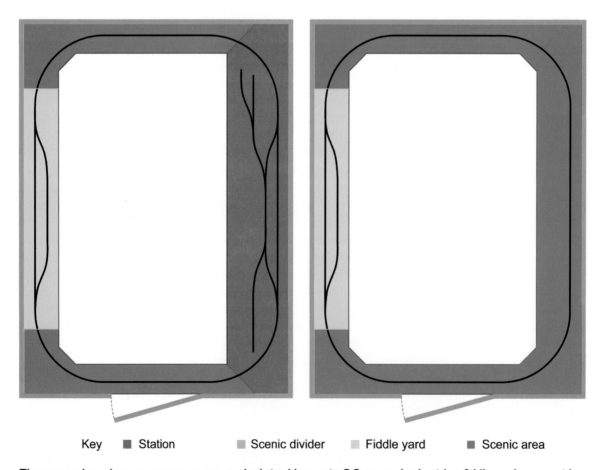

Key ■ Station   ■ Scenic divider   ■ Fiddle yard   ■ Scenic area

These two plans show an average room- or shed-sized layout in OO gauge, both with a fiddle yard on one side. The plan on the left is typical in that the other side is given over to the station, but this leaves just two short sections of open track. Dispensing with the station for the plan on the right gives a long continuous track with more opportunities for modelling the lineside.

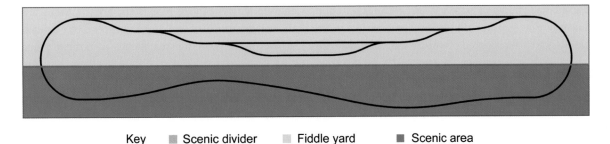

Key ■ Scenic divider ■ Fiddle yard ■ Scenic area

Long, thin layouts offer lots of opportunity for modelling the lineside and they are often long enough to include a station as well. They also allow for a high-capacity fiddle yard at the rear to hold lots of trains. Layouts like this could be mounted on a shelf, although access to the fiddle yard may be a problem; therefore, this is a design often adopted for exhibition layouts that allow access all round. Note how the track has formed a curvy line in the scenic section to avoid mirroring the obviously long and thin appearance of the baseboard.

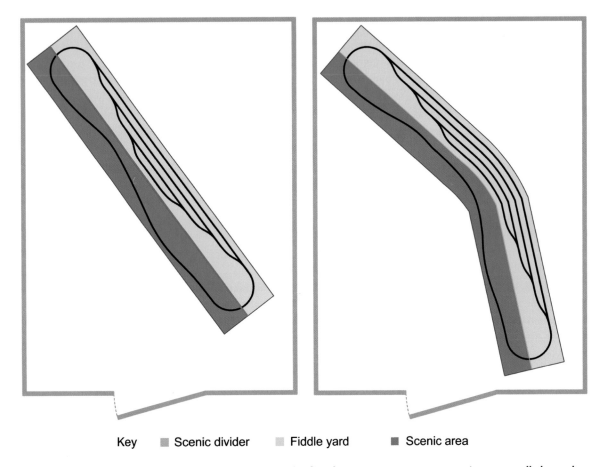

Key ■ Scenic divider ■ Fiddle yard ■ Scenic area

A long, thin layout with lots of lineside potential can be fitted into an average room against one wall, down the middle, or, as shown in the plan on the left, at a diagonal. This will maximize its length, but still requires a gap to access the fiddle yard at the rear. Introducing a kink in the middle as shown in the plan on the left makes better use of the available space. It still allows access all round the layout, but delivers a longer length of lineside potential.

decent-sized fiddle yard for a layout without a station since all that you can do is watch the trains go by. Unless you are prepared to watch the same train go past all the time, you need a way to change the train quickly without having to stop it and take one lot of rolling stock off the rails and replace it with another set. Therefore, a large fiddle yard with lots of storage tracks is a must.

The fiddle yard is not a scenic proposition, but you cannot live without it if you want to have a steady stream of trains passing through the scenic part of the layout. The classic room-based layout has the fiddle yard on one side and the station on the other; by not having a station, you can achieve a reasonable main line on one side of the room.

Another option is to put the fiddle yard immediately behind the layout. This works well in the smaller scales such as N gauge, where the 180-degree loops at each end that join the front to the back are much smaller. This approach is often seen on exhibition layouts where there is room at the back for the operators and room at the front for the spectators; however, it is not an arrangement that will suit all situations for home-based layouts.

Do not be restricted to traditional thinking. By placing a long, thin layout with the fiddle yard at the rear on the diagonal within a room, a longer straight run can be achieved. A further variation is to introduce a slight kink in the middle to create a sort of boomerang shape. Such layouts effectively sit in the middle of the room, which makes it easier to have all-round access to both the fiddle yard and the scenic portion.

Although you want to maximize the scenic portion in relation to the trains, you can only see the trains from one vantage point at a time. Rather than having a layout which is a series of small scenes through which long trains travel (and thus dominate the scene), consider having just one big scene in which the train can be seen in its entirety.

PASSING LOOPS

One operation that a sizeable station permits is the ability for one train to pass another. Fast passenger trains catch up with the slower ones and would be held up if they cannot pass them. Freight trains are an even greater problem, since they tend to be much slower (more so in the steam era than in the modern era). If you discard the station altogether from the layout design, trains cannot pass each other in the same direction.

The railways faced a similar problem, in that there were not enough sizeable stations along the line to cope with a large mix of fast and slow trains. Major routes had fast and slow lines side by side, but most railway lines could not justify such expenditure on infrastructure. The answer was the strategic placement of passing loops so that trains could overtake one another.

Given that even a large model railway can only ever represent a small portion of a railway line, there is no real need to have any passing loops. Certainly, it is unlikely that fast trains will need to overtake slow ones on the very short distance from the fiddle yard. However, passing loops will make a very interesting feature, not least for all the lineside infrastructure that they require. As a minimum, passing loops will require signals to control the train movements safely and a signal box to control the signals themselves. In the steam era, there may have been water cranes supplied by a water tower in order to replenish thirsty steam locomotives.

GOING SEPARATE WAYS

Most of the infrastructure required for passing loops would also be found at junctions. Not all junctions were to be found at stations; they were often in the middle of nowhere, but where it was convenient to branch off in different directions. The diverging tracks might actually run in parallel for a short while, which makes it easier to lead both lines to the same destination on your model railway, namely, the fiddle yard.

There would be quite an array of signals, possibly using a signal gantry if space was tight, as might be the case in the cramped confines of an urban environment. There would probably be a platelayers' hut close by, as regular inspection and maintenance of the turnouts and signals at the junction would be vital.

Double-track main lines diverge in this scene on 'Glazebrook', the N-gauge exhibition layout of the Warrington Model Railway Club. Although there is a road (and convenient road bridges to hide the entrance to the fiddle yard), this is a scene that is very much in the middle of the countryside, with nothing around. Note the different types of boundary fencing, as well as signals and numerous telegraph poles.

OUT IN THE COUNTRY

By a fair margin, the most popular setting represented by model railways is a rural one, especially when representing a portion of the railway line between two major destinations. The green space between railway centres constitutes the majority of track, often for many miles between stations and junctions.

This leaves a fair amount of property for the railways to look after. Often this property is hard to access without roads nearby, one of the reasons for the proliferation of platelayers' huts along the line in the steam era, as local track gangs could work their area from their hut.

In many ways, the lineside running through the countryside is quite bland and featureless. There may be some bridges, but in real life it is the landscape that is the defining feature. There is still a challenge to the railway modeller to capture the atmosphere of the lineside authentically in miniature. After all, the lineside is part of the stage that is really there to showcase the trains themselves.

INNER CITY

Compared to the countless miles of railway running through fields and hills, the tracks that run through towns and cities amount to quite a small proportion of the whole. Yet this landscape, thoroughly urban with little or no greenery, is a very different place indeed. The contrast between brick and grass could not be more extreme.

The railways still needed to protect their boundaries from trespass, but in the concrete jungle, things

'Marston Magna' is a superb recreation of a section of the Westbury to Weymouth line in the 1950s by the West Camel Model Railway Club. The use of N gauge allows the space to set the railway line truly into the landscape, so that the pleasure is to be found in watching the trains pass through that landscape. Lineside features to note include a platelayers' hut, telegraph poles, a signal and wooden lineside fencing.

STEVE FLINT (COURTESY RAILWAY MODELLER)

Ian Clark's OO gauge layout 'Rockingham' is set in South Yorkshire in 1929. In this representation of a semi-urban industrial location, it is just as important to protect the railway from accidental trespass. This has been achieved with wooden lineside fencing and a traditional gated level crossing. STEVE FLINT (COURTESY RAILWAY MODELLER)

often had to be more substantial. This meant a lot more use of brick walls to mark the boundary, or retaining walls to keep the earth in its place through cuttings.

The demarcation of the boundary is often more obvious in an urban environment, since in the towns and cities land is at a premium. The railway is often cheek by jowl with the urban setting it serves. Houses are the most prevalent, either with the yards of terraced housing backing on to the railway, or streets running alongside with houses and flats behind.

Ironically, the modern railway often seems less compressed in an urban environment than it did in the past. This is because rationalization and contraction have reduced the amount of railway; double tracks are singled, fast and slow lines merged into one. This leaves quite a spacious border by the side of the remaining railway lines. A modern layout could feature an abandoned line beside the remaining line. An interesting feature would be a multi-arched bridge, one arch having track while the other arch does not.

CHAPTER TWO

DEFINING THE BOUNDARY

The railways were huge property owners. A colossal amount of the initial investment to build a railway would have been spent to acquire the land. Railways are long and thin, but they still amount to quite a lot of land. Not surprisingly, the original railway companies were keen to protect their investment and to demonstrate to the public that, basically, a railway line is private property.

The first rule of private property is: no trespassing. Railways have always been keen to deter trespass on their land, either intentional or accidental. People often need to be protected from themselves and wandering across railway tracks has always been (and remains) a dangerous pastime. You might think that you will hear and see a train coming. In the steam era, it was true that a dirty big clanking locomotive would announce its presence a long way off. The modern era is very different and trains (especially electric ones) can be virtually silent. This is why British Railways started painting the ends of locomotives yellow so that they could be seen from a distance after an increasing number of fatalities to trackworkers (used to noisy steam locomotives), who just did not hear the new trains coming.

It is not just humans who need to be kept off the tracks; four-legged creatures can cause a lot of chaos as well and as they are generally in pursuit of the tastiest grass, they are no respecters of the finer points of property ownership. The accidental death of livestock at the hands of the railway could lead to some interesting claims for compensation. In rare cases, large animals can even derail a train, as happened when a train hit a cow at Polmont in Scotland – the driving coach was lighter than a locomotive and so derailed, with serious consequences.

It will come as no surprise therefore that as the railways have always taken their boundaries seriously, there are a large number of ways to protect them.

These ways largely fall into either walls or fences, but there is a huge variety within each of these categories. This is good news for the modeller, as it means that you are spoilt for choice. Sometimes a specific type of boundary is necessary if you really want to define a time and place and there are plenty of options for this. Otherwise, you can take your pick as to how you want your railway to look. Never forget that it is your railway and ultimately you can do as you please. Above all else, these ways to mark the edge of the railway's domain quite clearly define the edge of the lineside.

WOODEN FENCING

The wooden fence is the most traditional and popular form of boundary to be used by the railway. It was extremely common in the steam era; indeed, some styles of fencing are directly associated with certain railway companies. Wooden fencing is less commonly used on today's railway, as although it is sufficient to keep animals out, it is not much of a challenge to humans. Preserved railways, however, often still use wooden fencing to define their boundary, not least because it is in keeping with the era that they try to recreate.

Wooden fencing can be thought of as traditional farming field fencing. This consists of vertical posts set fairly close together with a number of horizontal bars between the posts. Timber tended to be cheap and plentiful, so such fencing is an economical option for the miles and miles of open track.

KITS FOR WOODEN 'FARM' FENCING

As a reflection of how important and common the simple wooden fence is for defining the real railway's boundary, there are probably more kits for this than anything else in the entire model railway hobby. All the major scales are amply provided for, so there is no difficulty in finding what you want for your particular model railway situation. Prices are all broadly similar, though some packs will go further than others, so it is worth measuring first of all to see how much model fencing you will need and then work out a final price. Most manufacturers publish how much fencing is in their packs.

Peco's Flexible Field Fencing kits have been available for many years and they have a lot going for them. First of all, they are available in each of the three major modelling scales, namely, N gauge, OO gauge and O gauge. They are moulded in a fairly generic brown plastic, which looks acceptable but would benefit from a coat of paint or matt varnish.

The Peco range is called 'flexible' because it is just that. There is a tendency for many fencing kits only to make fencing in pretty much a straight line on the level. The real world is not always straight and flat. Where the horizontal bars of Peco's fencing are attached to the vertical posts, the plastic is a little bit thinner. This means that it will easily bend both in the horizontal and vertical planes. Therefore, going round corners and climbing up hills is really easy.

The Peco fencing comes with spigots moulded under the posts for attaching the fencing to the layout. So it is a simple case of drilling holes to accept these spigots. By choosing a drill bit that matches the diameter of the spigots, the fencing can be installed with nothing more than an interference fit; no potentially messy glue is needed. Measuring the location of the holes is easy, because you can use the fencing itself as a template.

Peco also offers a 'fences and gates' pack in OO gauge, marketed under the Model Scene Accessories brand. This pack is perhaps intended more for farmers' fields, but it is worth remembering that fencing is fencing and that there is virtually no difference between the post and bar fencing used by farmers and that used by railway companies. Indeed, the railway's boundary often butts up against farming land, so is it railway fencing or is it farm fencing?

The Model Scene Accessories product is again moulded in brown plastic that would benefit from a coat of paint or matt varnish. It is not as flexible as the Peco product, though as individual panels on the sprue, it can at least be made to go around corners. Rather than fixing spigots, the panels have small feet at the bottom, so if you are not so sure about being

Peco's Flexible Field Fencing is available in all the main modelling scales. This N-gauge layout shows a run of the fencing at the top of a shallow cutting and ably illustrates how the flexibility of the plastic allows it to hug the undulating terrain, curving and climbing and even doing both at the same time.

Some fencing products come with moulded bases to help keep it upright, as with the piece shown at the front made by Model Scene Accessories. While the bases make the fencing easy to install, they do not look very realistic; however, once a layer of ground cover is applied, as seen with the two pieces at the rear, the bases are soon disguised.

able to drill holes for the fence posts, this product is really easy to install, since the feet can just be glued to the baseboard. You may think that plastic feet will look unsightly and unrealistic; however, it is a simple matter to disguise them with ground cover when adding the scenery.

It is possible to add fences after all the scenic work has been completed. You may be tempted to do it this way, perhaps fearing that the fences will get in the way, or be damaged while adding the scenery, but measuring and drilling holes for posts is a lot easier to do on a blank baseboard. The holes required for fence posts can be so small that there is a tendency to lose sight of them in the greenery once the drill bit is removed.

Another major manufacturer of fencing is Ratio Plastic Models, with a range of products covering both N gauge and OO gauge. In N gauge, it produces lineside fencing in either 'wood brown' or white. The moulding is very fine, as is appropriate for the smaller scale. It is not 'flexible' per se, but the bars are thin enough to be persuaded to go around corners and up modest inclines.

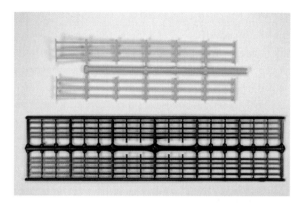

The most popular modelling scale is OO gauge, not least because it is easy to model most things to scale, including the posts and bars of wooden fencing. Both the products shown here (Dapol at the top, Ratio Plastic Models at the bottom) would look realistic on a layout. Being plastic, there is a little bit of give in the mouldings to follow curves in the track, although going up or down hills would be hard without cutting the bars from the posts, trimming and then reattaching.

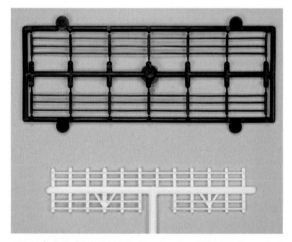

Wooden fencing for N gauge can be harder to manufacture for the smaller scale so as to get the posts and bars looking fine enough. The black Ratio Plastic Models fencing at the top is finely moulded, while the white Kestrel Designs fencing at the bottom is a bit more chunky. Real fencing comes in all shapes and sizes, often dependent upon the wood to hand, so both products are suitable for N gauge.

For OO gauge modellers, Ratio Plastic Models produces lineside fencing in black or white plastic. These packs come in decent lengths, though the plastic is quite substantial, which limits its flexibility, and there are no spigots under the posts for fixing.

Exclusively for N gauge modellers are the products from Kestrel Designs. The range includes lineside fencing in either white or brown. The moulding is a little bit basic and tricky to get off the sprues, but the variety of sections on the sprue makes this a useful product for modellers of the smaller scale.

Still available after decades of production is an OO gauge kit of fences and gates originally produced by Kitmaster and now available from Dapol. The kit is moulded in grey plastic, so painting is a must. The posts have very small spigots underneath that could be fitted into pre-drilled holes, but really they are meant to go into discrete plastic bases that feature a gravel effect on top. This is a good, solid product that has graced thousands of layouts and the separate base pieces provide a choice of how to fix it to the baseboard.

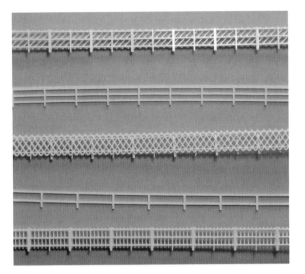

It is hard to believe that this wide range of different types of fencing manufactured by York Modelmaking is actually produced for the smallest commercial model railway scale, namely N gauge. While some of the more ornate types are perhaps more appropriate for stations, there is something here for everyone's tastes. The use of very thin sheet plastic and accurate laser cutting means that the fencing is flexible yet durable.

An exciting new manufacturing process that has gained prominence in the last ten years is laser cutting. This uses a laser to fret out parts from sheet materials such as plywood, MDF and plastic. A range of fencing is available from York Modelmaking. The laser cutting process is capable of producing very fine fencing for the smaller scales and the use of plastic for the material means that it is very flexible, so going round corners and up hills is easy.

While some of these fencing products are more rugged than others, it is inevitable that occasionally one of the bars will get broken in the middle, or where it meets the post. Real fencing does fall into disrepair over time, left at the mercy of the elements. Therefore, the odd bit of broken fencing does not look completely out of place; indeed, you can even deliberately break a bit of the fencing here and there. Do bear in mind, though, that the fencing served an important purpose in preventing trespass and for that reason the railway companies would have kept their fencing in good repair. It might have got broken, but it would not have stayed that way for very long.

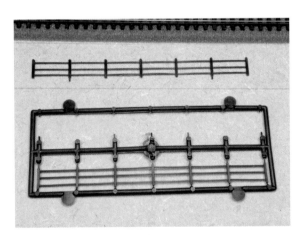

ABOVE LEFT: The first step when installing wooden fencing from a kit such as this N-gauge one by Ratio Plastic Models is to draw a line to work to that is parallel to the track. Each post of the fence has a spigot, but it is not necessary to use every one. In this case, the second and sixth posts are sufficient and the other spigots can be cut off when removing the piece from the sprue.

ABOVE RIGHT: Drill the first hole on the pencil line. A Vernier gauge is a useful but not essential tool, as it allows you to measure accurately the diameter of the spigot under the fence posts. Alternatively, start with a small drill bit and keep moving to the next size up until the spigot fits into the hole.

ABOVE LEFT: Time taken to match the size of the hole in the baseboard to the size of the spigot will be well spent, since it means that an interference fit can be achieved. This means that no glue is required, which makes it quicker and cleaner to install the fencing pieces.

ABOVE RIGHT: With the first spigot inserted into a hole in the baseboard, use the fence piece to see where the second hole should be drilled. This second hole needs to be quite accurately placed, or else the fence piece will bow or stretch. If in doubt, mark the location of the hole with a pencil and then check that the spigot lines up exactly before drilling the hole.

The fence pieces in most kits are complete, in the sense that there is a post at each end. This means that when two pieces are placed next to each other, there is a double post. In most cases, this does not look too obvious, especially in the smaller scales. Alternatively, cut off the post on one piece and butt the crosspieces to the other post (a little glue may sometimes be necessary).

SCRATCH-BUILT WOODEN 'FARM' FENCING

Given the plethora of kits that are available in all the major railway modelling scales, you may wonder why anyone would even contemplate scratch-building wooden fencing. One potential issue with the kits is that they are all made from injection-moulded plastic.

No matter how you try, plastic looks like plastic, not wood. All but the darkest plastics have a slightly shiny finish to them and those moulded in brown to represent treated wood are perhaps the worst offenders. You can paint the plastic kits; a nice matt finish will look much more realistic. However, all those posts and bars require a lot of effort with a paintbrush (airbrushing would speed things up enormously, especially if you have a large layout with a lot of fencing).

If you really want your fencing to look like wood, then you might as well use wood to make it. Balsa wood and strip wood are available in a variety of thicknesses and sizes; do not restrict yourself to model railway suppliers for these materials, as you are more likely to find what you want in a shop that caters for model boat or aircraft builders.

Building a wooden fence out of real wood probably only comes into its own for those modelling in the larger scales, such as O gauge and above. You could use matchsticks in OO gauge, but it could be rather fiddly (plain match wood can also be bought for modelling without the need to strike a lot of matches). Any glue can be used to build the fence, although balsa wood cement or white woodworking glue are the best.

Real wood is best treated with the required colour before assembly. Paint is an option, but then you might as well just paint a plastic fence kit. Real wood can be stained with actual wood preservatives and finishes, or a wash of India ink diluted with isopropyl alcohol.

Scratch-building a fence really allows the fence to be moulded to the landscape. If you are modelling flat, open land, there is really not much advantage here and it could become rather boring and time-consuming building several scale miles of fencing. It really comes into its own on rockier ground, such as might be found in Scotland, or on a Welsh narrow-gauge line. In these situations, the fencing can really be made to hug the contours, something that is a lot harder to do with most fencing kits.

If you want really bespoke lineside fencing but without using real wood, you can scratch-build it using plastic strip. There are several manufacturers, for example Plastruct and Evergreen Scale Models, who make a range of round and rectangular strip in every conceivable thickness. Plastic strip is very easy to work with. Thin strip cuts easily, while liquid polystyrene cement can be brushed on and dries quickly, which means you can work very rapidly. In order

to cut lots of similarly sized pieces of plastic strip, consider investing in one of the so-called 'choppers', which are like a miniature guillotine; set the guide and feed in the plastic strip to produce lots of identical cuts. The end result will, though, need to be painted.

If a lot of the scratch-built fencing will be to a regular shape and size, consider making yourself a simple jig to speed up construction. A few track pins nailed into a piece of wood or thick card are all that is needed. These serve as a simple physical guide for where to place the pieces as well as holding things in place. The fencing will be flimsy to start with until all the pieces are glued on.

One final option for scratch-built fencing is to use card stock, especially a good-quality artist's material. The outline of the fence can be drawn on to the card in fine pencil and a sharp craft knife and a steel ruler used to cut out between the bars and posts. A good-quality card will stand being cut such that the posts and bars can be quite thin. Choosing a card that is up to 1mm thick will give the posts and beams a realistic thickness.

A much thinner card could be used if the fencing was towards the rear of a layout, say at the top of an embankment, where it would be less obvious

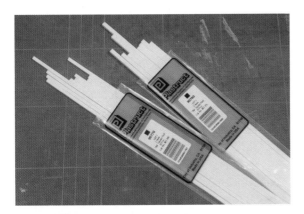 

ABOVE LEFT: Bespoke scratch-built wooden 'farm' fencing is easily catered for thanks to the wide range of packs of plastic strip available from the likes of Plastruct. You can select different-sized square sections to represent the posts and the crosspieces. Being plastic, these products are easy to work with and simple to join together using a liquid polystyrene cement.

ABOVE RIGHT: If you are going to scratch-build a lot of fencing, it is best to make a simple jig in order to speed up what is basically a very repetitive modelling process. Start by drawing three pairs of parallel lines to represent the crosspieces. Use an actual piece of the square plastic section selected for the crosspieces to mark each pair of lines.

 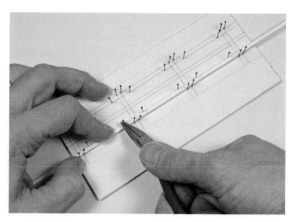

ABOVE LEFT: Draw in the posts, again using a piece of the square plastic section selected to mark each pair of lines. Then insert pins where the top and bottom crosspieces will join the posts. Small pins are best for this job and track pins such as these Peco ones are ideal. If you use cardboard as the base for the template, the pins can be pushed in using pliers.

ABOVE RIGHT: Add additional pins to hold the crosspieces in place. Note how a piece of the plastic strip is being used to check that the pins are inserted in exactly the right place.

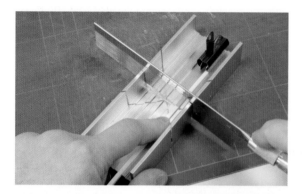 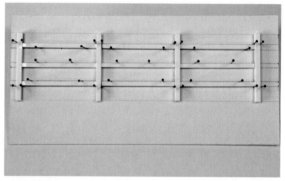

ABOVE LEFT: Accurately cutting large quantities of plastic strip for fence posts and crosspieces is quickly achieved by using a razor saw in a metal mitre block. Note the use of a small bulldog clip as a stop. This means it is only necessary to measure once and then the stop ensures that every piece is exactly the same length.

ABOVE RIGHT: This view shows a completed section of fencing for an O gauge layout. Always apply glue sparingly to avoid sticking the fencing to the jig. To add subsequent sections of fencing to this one, you would omit either the left- or right-hand post and glue the crosspieces from the next section to the post of the current section.

The completed fencing can be installed on a layout. A piece of wire has been inserted into the base of alternate posts, which is then inserted into holes in the baseboard; this makes it easy to install the fencing, as well as making it slightly less prone to accidental damage. The white plastic has been painted with thinned washes of black and brown to give a slightly weathered 'creosoted' finish.

that it was thinner. It is possible to get thinner card through most PC-compatible home printers, having first drawn the design for the fencing using a simple CAD (Computer-Aided Design) or drawing package, which saves having to draw it out by hand.

You can even get PC-compatible machines for home use that replace the print head with a knife to literally cut it out for you. This requires a little bit of time to set up, but then you have an endless supply of fencing for just the price of a few sheets of card. As these devices cut very accurately time after time, several pieces of the thinner card could be laminated to get thicker posts and beams. Finally, by obtaining the right colour of brown card, you may also save yourself the effort of having to paint the completed fencing.

SLATTED WOODEN FENCING

Needless to say, wooden fencing does not just have to be of the 'farm' type with posts and vertical bars. Wood has always been a very flexible material and it can be nailed together in all shapes and sizes.

A common arrangement is to attach vertical pieces to the wooden bars between the posts. It is usual to leave gaps to let the wind through and use less material. This kind of fencing is often found more in urban situations than rural ones, where the population is larger and perhaps in need of more encouragement to stay off the railway's land.

The materials and techniques for scratch-building such fencing are the same as for 'farm' fencing. Even a few inches of this type of fencing will require a lot of individual pieces, but the effect in just a small area of urban modelling will be impressive. Such fencing often extends well above head-height to discourage fly-tipping 'over the fence'.

Ratio Plastic Models produces a kit of this type of wooden fencing in OO gauge. Being plastic, it will benefit from a coat of paint or varnish. This kind of fencing is quite rigid, so the plastic moulding is too; therefore, there is no chance of getting it to go around corners or up inclines. If your model requires such changes in direction, then scratch-building is the only real option.

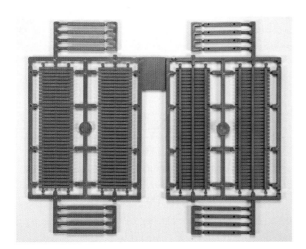 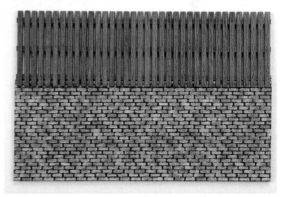

ABOVE LEFT: Ratio Plastic Models makes a very well-moulded plastic kit for slatted fencing. The colour is close to wood, though it would at least benefit from weathering and a coat of matt varnish. Although intended for OO gauge, it could conceivably be used as a very tall fence in N gauge and it certainly would not look out of place in O gauge as a lower fence.

ABOVE RIGHT: Some brick walls are extended upwards with simple wooden fencing in order to provide additional security, especially in urban environments. The slatted fencing by Ratio Plastic Models is ideal for this and an example is shown here atop a wall made from card coated with brick paper. Note how the plastic fencing has been given a wash of brown paint to both weather it and remove the plastic appearance.

One final suggestion for this type of fencing is to combine it with a low brick wall. In urban places where an existing wall is not enough to keep people and rubbish out it is often extended upwards with wooden fencing, perhaps bolstered with some supporting pieces of timber. The Ratio Plastic Models kit could easily be adapted and enhanced to sit atop a wall.

SLEEPER FENCING

Not surprisingly, the railways used vast quantities of sleepers to support the tens of thousands of miles of track. Sleepers have a lifespan, often starting out on the main line and then being relegated to sidings. Even when they are 'life-expired' in terms of supporting track, the timber is often still in quite good condition, hardly surprising given the amount of creosote that was pumped into them (usually under high pressure rather than just a wash with a paintbrush).

With a steady supply of pieces of reasonable quality timber all conveniently cut to the same length, it is understandable that the railway companies recycled their old sleepers by turning them into fencing. With a piece of timber or iron at the top to hold the planks in line, the result was a very solid fence indeed. Therefore, it was often found in places where heavy duty fencing was required, such as the Scottish Highlands or the Settle to Carlisle line. In such places it could serve a dual purpose, acting as fencing and as a means of limiting snowdrifts to keep snow off the lines.

You can purchase individual sleepers for making your own track and this is one option for making a sleeper fence, though it could be quite expensive. Strips of plastic card can be chopped into sleeper-sized lengths and this is likely to be a more cost-effective option. It is worth distressing the edges of the plastic strips with a knife and sandpaper to add some individual character to the resulting fence. Each sleeper should not be perfectly glued to its neighbour; a little variation in how upright the sleepers are will add character as well as making the edges between sleepers easier to see on the completed fence.

There is only one commercially available sleeper-type fencing in OO gauge and this is a plaster casting from Ten Commandments. The casting process means that it is only detailed on one side, but this is

Railways had a plentiful supply of used sleepers that they put to use building fences, ballast bins and unguarded crossings. This is an OO gauge plaster-cast model of some sleeper fencing made by Ten Commandments. All that is needed is a wash of brown paint to complete it.

not a problem if placed to the rear of the layout, or in such a way that the unfinished side cannot be seen. Being a plaster casting, there is absolutely no means of bending it round corners. It does have a clever little rebate at each end that will make it very easy to join successive pieces together on the straight.

P&D Marsh produces a white-metal kit that will give you about a foot of sleeper fencing in N gauge. This represents the type of sleeper fencing whereby the sleepers are laid horizontally between vertical sleepers used as posts. The softness of white metal means that it is possible to bend the castings a little at the posts in order to curve the fences in the horizontal plane (though not the vertical).

CONCRETE FENCING

While we may think that we live in a modern 'concrete jungle', concrete has in fact been employed as a building material for many years and its use certainly predates World War II. One of the big advantages of concrete is that it can be cast into shape using a mould; the result is a repeatable process producing identical components that are strong and need no maintenance (unlike wooden fencing, which requires painting). Of all the railway companies, perhaps the Southern Railway is most closely associated with the use of cast concrete, for everything from lamp posts to platelayers' huts, and of course, fencing.

Concrete has always made very good fence posts, especially if reinforced with steel wire inside the casting. Scratch-building concrete fence posts is no different to making 'wooden' ones by using lengths of plastic strip. The only difference is in the finish with a 'concrete-coloured' or pale grey paint.

Ratio Plastic Models produces a very useful kit of concrete fence posts in OO gauge. It is doubly good value because it includes a selection of warning signs as well. These posts have short spigots to attach to the baseboard. The modeller is left to source the wire to thread through the moulded holes in the post. While wire is the usual material, consider using thin plastic round rod. This is flexible enough to go around corners and up inclines, easy to cut to shape and it can be welded to the fence posts for strength using a liquid polystyrene cement (in a well-ventilated area).

Ratio Plastic Models also produces a kit of concrete fence panels in OO gauge, while Peco makes a similar kit in O gauge. As concrete fence panels are rather plain, the finishing is crucial to avoid a large expanse of fencing looking the same. Concrete does exhibit tonal variation as it ages and weathers, so avoid using the same colour all over. Mix in a bit of white or black to the main grey colour to get some variation. When the fence is finished, a wash of heavily thinned black will help to give it a 'stained' and weathered appearance.

Given that concrete panel fencing is so simple, it lends itself easily to scratch-building. Posts can once again be made from plastic strip, while the panels can

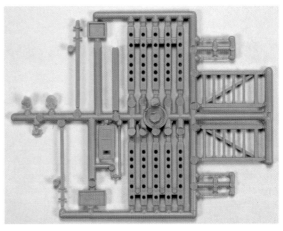

Concrete fence posts have been used by the railways since before nationalization and it was a material particularly favoured by the Southern Railway. The longevity of concrete as a material means that, where used, it is likely to have lasted a long time, possibly even to the present day. Ratio Plastic Models produces a plastic sprue with parts to represent concrete fencing, including gates and some very finely detailed warning signs. Brass wire or plastic rod can be used to represent the wire strung between the posts.

be cut from thin plastic sheet or even card. You will only see the texture of concrete when modelling in the larger scales, but, sometimes, cheaper card (without any shiny finish) will have just enough texture to represent concrete.

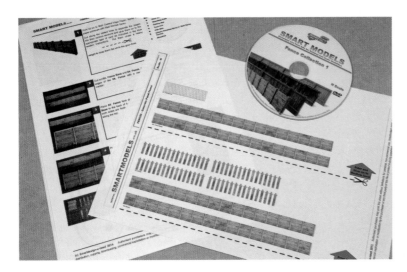

There are an increasing number of manufacturers offering card kits as either downloads from the Internet, or on a CD. The kit comes as a PDF file with instructions. The advantage is that you can print the kit yourself as many times as you want. If you need literally miles of fencing of a certain type, this could be a very economical option. The example shown here is concrete panel fencing in N gauge by Smart Models.

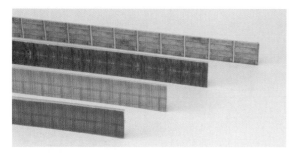

This shows the Smart Models N-gauge concrete fencing (at the rear) once it has been cut out and attached to a strip of cardboard. Any PVA-type glue will do the job, as will spray adhesive or double-sided sticky tape. The other three types of fencing shown are available on the same CD.

WIRE-IN-POST FENCING

Another variation of 'farm' fencing is the so-called wire-in-post fencing. There is no getting away from fence posts for fencing, but you can dispense with the wooden vertical bars and replace them with wire. The 'in-post' part logically refers to passing the wire through a hole in the post. One of the problems for modelling such fencing, especially in the smaller scales, is that it is difficult to represent the wire at anything like scale thickness. Some fencing does use a thicker wire that is more akin to bar than wire, but, generally, the wire used is very thin.

Model fence posts can be made from sections of plastic strip or real wood. These posts then require a number of holes to be drilled into them at a right angle. A pillar drill would ensure perfectly right-angled holes every time, but this is probably overkill. An electrically powered model drill will make life easier when drilling possibly hundreds of holes. One essential is a simple jig to make sure that the holes go in the same place every time.

There are various options for representing the wire. Real wire is strong, yet flexible. It is available as thin as 0.33in, which will look quite realistic in OO gauge, even N gauge. Some modellers have used cotton or similar thread to represent the wire, but it has several drawbacks. It needs to be kept taut to avoid it hanging like a thread, it can be tricky to feed through the holes in the fence posts and it can fray all too easily. Round plastic rod is available as thin as 0.1mm; in most respects it is similar to using wire, with the added advantage that you are able to weld plastic to plastic using liquid polystyrene cement.

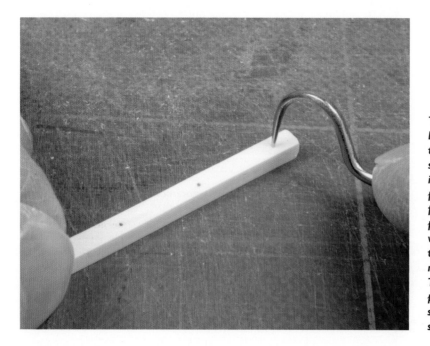

The starting point for scratch-building wire-in-post fencing is to source suitable square section in plastic or wood. This is Plastruct 3.2mm square plastic section, which is ideal for O gauge. Having cut the posts from the strips, mark where the wires will go and then use a dental probe to mark a dimple into the plastic. The dimple marked into the plastic makes it a lot easier to start the drill going on the thin strip material.

Shown here is a drill bit in a pin vice; however, for mass-producing a lot of fence posts, using an electric mini-drill would be a lot quicker. Choose a drill bit that is fractionally wider than the wire that will be used. This allows a little 'wriggle room' for the wire in case any of the holes are not drilled at exactly 90 degrees in both planes.

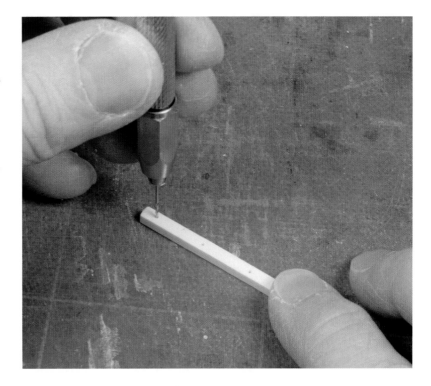

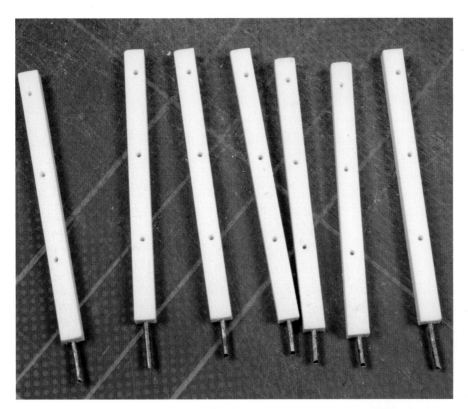

You can just glue the posts to the layout, but this would be very fragile indeed. One option is to make the posts much longer and fit them into pre-drilled holes (a square peg does fit into a round hole as long as they are the same size). Alternatively, as shown here, drill a hole in the base of the post and fit some stronger steel wire that can be fitted into a hole drilled into the baseboard.

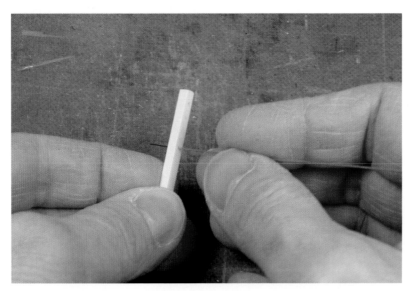

The wire used is 0.5mm brass and this simply feeds through the holes in the post. It may have a little bit of natural curve to it, but this is eliminated once the posts are secured to the layout. Gentle curves in the fencing are easy to introduce by setting the posts appropriately. More abrupt changes of direction and right-angled corners can be done by bending the wire. Going up gentle slopes is possible, but anything steeper would require the holes to be drilled at an appropriate angle.

The fence posts are easily installed on the layout by drilling equally spaced holes to accept the wire in the base of the posts. Do not worry about drilling the holes absolutely vertical; the wire can be bent as required until the posts are straight (although the occasional slightly leaning post adds a bit of character). The posts are painted a wash of black and brown to represent weathered creosote, while the wire is painted 'oily steel' to represent galvanized steel.

Plastic wire is available and this is what Ratio Plastic Models has included in its kit for OO gauge Great Western Railway (GWR) lineside fencing. The wire is glued to notches in the side of the post; once again, a liquid polystyrene glue will attach plastic to plastic. The resulting fencing is very fine and realistic, though this comes at the risk of being fragile. It is also an example of being able to buy a specific type of fencing as associated with a single railway company.

SECURITY FENCING

All fencing offers security in some way, but there are certain types of more modern fencing that are really designed to keep people out. Such fencing can be

Although modern era railways have not generally adopted the so-called 'chain link' fencing with concrete posts and their distinctive angled tops, such fencing can often be found where industrial premises butt up against the railway. Industrial sites value their security more than the railway, so they are happy to erect fencing to keep out thieves who would use the lineside for access. This OO gauge kit from Ratio Plastic Models includes well-moulded posts and even gates, although the latter would not be required by the lineside itself.

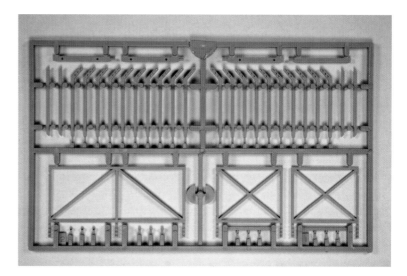

found defining the railway's boundary, though it may not necessarily be provided by the railway. Private premises often nestle by the side of a railway line and the owners may be concerned that people will try to access their site via the railway.

The most modern type of fencing is the so-called palisade fencing, a metal version of the wooden slatted fencing, though usually supplemented with some nasty-looking spikes on the top. This is sturdy stuff, often resistant even to some road vehicles. In model form, it can be scratch-built, but an awful lot of individual pieces of plastic strip would be required for even a modest length of fencing.

The best shortcut is to use the excellent kit from Knightwing International. This is made for OO gauge from plastic parts that are easily assembled. Spigots are provided for fixing to the baseboard, although discrete plastic bases are included as an easier alternative. The plastic is a mid-grey colour, but this type of fencing often looks metallic (sometimes it is painted or powder-coated, so choose whatever colour you prefer). A dull aluminium colour is probably best and it is easier to spray it on. An airbrush will help, although is not imperative; instead, you can try the extensive range of automotive paints in most car repair shops.

Ratio Plastic Models produces a plastic OO gauge kit of the slightly older type of security fencing, usually referred to as 'chain link' fencing. Such fencing has

distinctive concrete fence posts with a 45-degree angle at the top that usually holds two or three lengths of wire, or even barbed wire. This kit has to be built in situ, so it may be worth painting the parts beforehand, even though the plastic is almost concrete colour. Some very fine plastic mesh is included to represent the chain links.

The same type of fencing is also available in kit form for OO gauge modellers from Ten Commandments. This time, the fence posts are finely cast in white metal, with holes all the way up the posts for supporting wire, and some fine mesh is included to represent the chain links.

Despite the ease of use of these kits, you could scratch-build your own security fencing. Making the posts is simple, once again using lengths of plastic strip. For the chain links, try the car repair shops again, as they sell some very fine meshes that are intended for mending dents and holes in car bodywork.

STONE WALLING

A wide array of stone walling can be found. Stone walls can be cemented together like brick walls, although true 'dry' stone walling relies on the skill of the builder to place the stones together in such a way that no mortar is needed. Like the company-specific fencing that can define a time and place, stone walling can be unique to an area, thus helping to set the location. A number of products are available to the modeller who wishes to have stone walling to define the railway boundary.

STONE-WALL PRODUCTS

There are a number of different wall types in the Hornby Skaledale range in OO gauge (also Lyddle End in N gauge), from the generic 'granite wall' to the more specific 'Cotswold stone wall'. These are so-called 'ready-to-plant' items, since they are finished products; all you have to do is take them out of the packet and 'plant' them on your layout. They are made from resin castings that are ready-painted and the finishing effects are quite impressive. Straight sections and 90-degree corners are included in each pack.

There are two issues with using the Hornby products. Firstly, they are quite expensive (as you are paying for a finished product) and the cost could be prohibitive if you require a lot of wall. Secondly, they tend to be manufactured as a batch and when they have been sold, no more are made, so obtaining all the necessary pieces may be a problem if they have been on the market for a while.

Ancorton Models manufactures a range of stone walling for N gauge that is highly detailed and features a range of shapes (straights, curves and even damaged walling). This product is made from a lamination

of two pieces of laser-etched plywood that is then painted grey. The level of detail is excellent and, being made of wood, the sections can easily be cut to the required length.

Ten Commandments makes a section of stone walling that is nicely cast in plaster. It is supplied unpainted, but this means that it can be finished as required; for example, using thinned acrylics, enamels or watercolours on plaster gives a simple yet excellent finish. The colour of stone in a wall often reflects the locality of the place from which it was quarried, so if you want to represent a specific place, you can do no better than to paint it yourself.

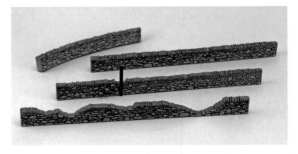

Ancorton Models produces some stone-wall sections in N gauge that are laser-cut and etched on thin plywood. The straight sections and curved pieces should cater for most basic track geometry. Once again, as a completely finished product, the price could be high if needed for a long stretch of track.

The extensive Hornby Skaledale range of OO gauge ready-to-plant buildings also includes a selection of stone-wall pieces with different finishes to represent different parts of the country. The detail and finish are outstanding, though the joints between pieces might need to be disguised with filler. You are also restricted to straight lines and right angles, while the price could be prohibitive for anything other than a short length of track.

Ten Commandments produces a very good plaster casting of a length of random stone wall. In its unpainted form, the plaster may well be representative of the stone found in some locations in the UK, but, generally, modellers will wish to paint the casting. Use washes of suitable grey colours; heavily thinned paints (enamel or acrylic) will soak into the plaster, resulting in different tones over the whole wall. Individually picking out a few stones in a different colour will also add interest.

Also requiring to be painted are the stone-wall sections produced in light grey plastic by Model Scene Accessories. These mouldings are a little bit basic by modern standards, but careful finishing will lift them above the ordinary. Start by painting the wall an overall base colour, then use a fine brush to pick out a few stones. As the moulded stones are quite big, this is easy to do using a fine paintbrush. You can mix white or black into your base colour to get shades above and below the overall colour, or pick a totally different colour; after all, stone walls can be quite random and possibly source their material from different quarries.

Once all the paint is dry, you can apply a mortar wash. This wash is a thinned paint of light grey (not white). Watercolours and acrylics can be thinned with water, and enamels with brush cleaner (thinners). Use a broad brush to 'wash' over the wall, then use a rag to wipe the surface of the wall. The rag will remove the paint from the stones, but leave it in the 'cracks' between stones. When it dries, you will have a mortar effect.

This technique does require some practice, not least in the thinning of the paint. This is crucial,

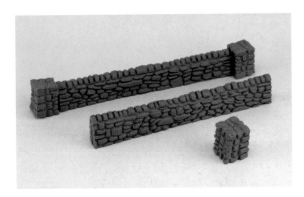

Model Scene Accessories produces a small pack of plastic moulded stone wall complete with corner towers that make it easy to produce right-angled enclosures. The suitably coloured grey plastic would benefit from some painting to avoid an unrealistic uniformity of colour. It can be much improved by a wash of light grey into the mortar lines to represent the mortar itself, as well as randomly picking out a few stones in different colours. In real life, stone can have quite a variety of shades of grey.

since if the paint is thinned too much, the rag will soak all the paint off, while if it is not thinned enough, the paint can dry on to the stones. Try it out on a scrap piece, or on one side of a wall that will not be obviously visible when installed on the layout.

SCRATCH-BUILT STONE WALLS

As with the wooden fencing, one of the problems with the products for stone walling is that it can be hard to make them go around corners and up hills. If you require a more complicated shape for your stone walls, scratch-building is certainly an option. There are a number of options open to you.

If you are particularly masochistic, you could build a wall stone by stone using individual stones made from an air-drying modelling clay such as that produced by DAS. This is probably more suited to the larger scales such as O gauge, where the fine detail can be seen and where only a small amount of walling is required.

A much easier and quicker method is to use the DAS modelling clay to form the basic shape of the wall. The clay can be rolled out and then cut into strips that can be persuaded around corners and up inclines. Modelling clays are quite easy to scribe with a sharp tool. It is easiest to do this before the clay fully hardens, when the surface is still a little soft. You can scribe by hand; things do not have to be too neat, as the stones are meant to be fairly random. When the clay is fully dry, the wall can be painted.

There are numerous 'stone-effect' sheets available to the modeller, either as moulded plastic sheet or as printed papers. Some even glory in descriptive names like 'rubble wall'. These sheets are easy to cut to the required shape and all they need is a core to which they can be applied. Thick card is ideal, but also consider corrugated cardboard. This is available for free from packaging and it is easy to curve. Cut a strip of cardboard with the grooves in the vertical and then drag it between thumb and forefinger to introduce a curve. Another material that is very light and easy to cut is foamboard (this has a polystyrene centre faced either side with thin card).

You can use various adhesives to stick the stone-wall sheets to the core, though be aware that paper sheets are just like wallpaper and that if you use a glue that is too 'wet' you may get rips or bubbles. A simple alternative is to use double-sided sticky tape.

Most walls need capping and this can be done with individual pieces of card, or by wrapping the sheet over the top of the core. The latter approach also helps to avoid unsightly gaps.

BRICK WALLS

Unlike stone walls, brick was a much less commonly used material for defining the railway boundary. It was even rarer to find it out in rural areas and it is almost exclusively found in towns and cities, where robust and hardworking construction were the order of the day. Brick walls clearly and safely defined the boundary, often at the end of a street of terraced houses, or perhaps protecting an alleyway running at the rear of houses.

Brick walls can vary considerably in height, which is perhaps why no manufacturer makes brick walls; however, they are very easy to scratch-build, as there is a wide selection of brick finishes in all the major scales. These are either printed on to paper (and thus are ready coloured), or are made from plastic sheet. Making the walls is the same as described for the stone walling and also as for making the largest of walls, the retaining wall.

RETAINING WALLS

The world is very rarely flat, but railways prefer the world to be flat. In order to achieve this as much as possible, railways elevate above the datum level using embankments, or push through the land that is above datum by means of a cutting. Where the railways have enough space, the slopes of the embankments and cuttings are wide enough that they do not need any support. In the usually more cramped conditions of towns and cities, there is not enough room for the slopes, so the land is 'retained' using a wall.

A retaining wall serves to fulfil the requirements of civil engineering, while also defining the railway boundary and acting as a barrier to trespass. Most retaining walls would win few architectural awards, by being largely plain expanses of brick or stone. These tend to be broken up by two things. Firstly, there are buttresses that help to provide additional strength. Secondly, some walls use a series of arches to join buttresses, the resulting shape being infilled with brick or stone.

READY-MADE RETAINING WALLS

There are quite a few kits and parts for retaining walls available from manufacturers, mostly in OO gauge and N gauge. Real retaining walls are, in a way, modular in construction, since they consist of repeating sections of arches or buttresses. This uniformity makes it easy for manufacturers to make these kits.

In the ready-to-plant area, there is a lovely range of retaining walls from Hornby Skaledale (OO gauge) and Lyddle End (N gauge). These represent brick and the finish is superb. They also feature a series of gently sloping walls that when linked together could support a gradient that runs from ground level to cross the main line via a bridge.

Ten Commandments makes a series of stone walls of differing heights in OO gauge. These plaster-cast panels can be joined to make long retaining walls. Included in the range are end pillars, to which can be joined left-hand or right-hand sloping pieces to represent the start or finish of the wall. These pieces also cleverly join the two heights of available wall so that a change in height can be achieved partway along the wall.

Gaugemaster produces some very substantial stone retaining walls with arches for OO gauge. These are made from a very dense foam material, which makes them quite light for their size and bulk; this could be a consideration for portable layouts.

Ratio Plastic Models produces stone-arched retaining wall kits in OO gauge and N gauge. These are made from plastic to the usual extremely high standard of fidelity. The OO gauge kit includes pillars that help to hide the joins between panels.

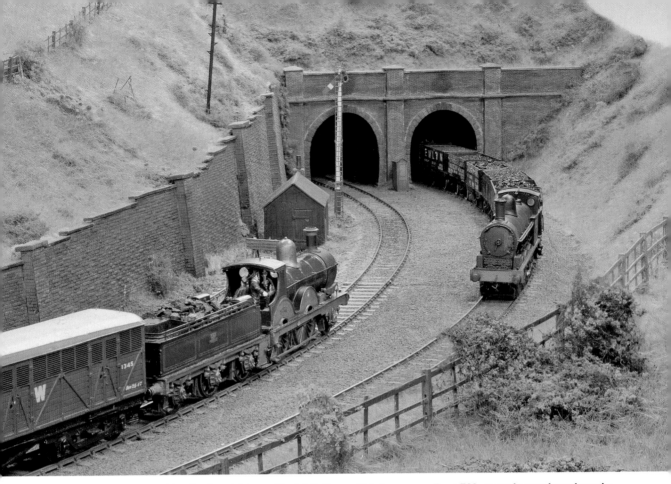

'Hope-under-Dinmore' by the South Hants Model Railway Club is a marvellous EM gauge layout based on the Shrewsbury to Hereford line in the first part of the twentieth century. This scene shows the classic use of a simple retaining wall, namely the approach to a tunnel. Note also the telegraph pole, platelayers' hut, signal and wooden fencing. CRAIG TILEY (COURTESY RAILWAY MODELLER)

The Hornby OO gauge Skaledale range of cast-resin structures includes a selection of superbly detailed and finished retaining walls. Various linked pieces are made to produce quite a long run that inclines from ground level to well above the trains. All that is needed is simply to install the pieces on to your layout. The joins between pieces can be disguised with foliage or thin plastic tube to represent drainage pipes.

Gaugemaster makes a chunky stone-effect retaining wall piece, which is moulded in a dense but lightweight foam. This might be important if you have a portable layout, where overall weight could be an issue. The unpainted foam would benefit from having some of the stones picked out in differing shades for variety and a wash of a mortar-coloured paint to highlight the courses between the stones. Some overall weathering such as soot stains would really make this an outstanding retaining wall.

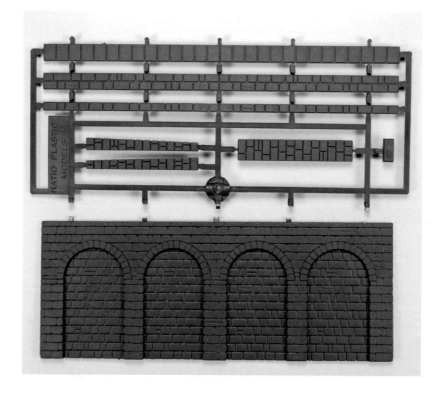

Ratio Plastic Models makes a kit in both OO gauge and N gauge for an arched stone retaining wall. These are very simple kits to build. The basic dark grey plastic is a good base for painting and finishing. You can pick whatever colour is appropriate for the local stone of the area you are modelling. A wash for the mortar courses and some weathering will produce a very realistic retaining wall.

Hiding the joins can be a problem, as you do not want a retaining wall to appear to have a huge crack from top to bottom. Well-fitting parts will help and most wall panels are designed so that pillars form the join between sections. As these pillars extend outwards, this helps to disguise the join. If all else fails, a small amount of model filler can be used to fill the gap, especially on kits that need painting anyway.

SCRATCH-BUILT RETAINING WALLS

While you might not be confident enough to make a building of a station or a house from scratch, by comparison building a retaining wall is really easy. By cutting your teeth on a simple project you will learn skills and gain the practice to tackle something more ambitious, like a house.

The starting point is to choose your wall covering and in this respect the modeller is extremely well catered for. Various styles of brick and stone paper are available from Metcalfe Models, Superquick, Smart Models and Scalescenes (the latter two are downloadable PDF files that you can print yourself as many times as you want). Peco and Ratio Plastic Models provide some very stout sheets of plastic brick or stone, though these are quite small pieces and difficult to cut with a knife due to being quite thick. Slater's Plastikard produces a range of thin plastic card sheets of various styles that are easy to cut and work with.

Most of these products are available in the major commercial scales from O gauge down to N gauge and are obviously suitable for any scale in-between. It is worth mentioning that while bricks are always the same size, stones in stone walls are less so. This means that a stone-effect paper or plastic sheet for one scale may be suitable for either a larger scale or a smaller scale than the one stated.

While thin plastic card is simple to cut with a knife into broadly rectangular shapes, cutting arches and pillars is a bit trickier. If you are relatively new to modelling, the paper-effect coverings are much easier to work with. Some modellers are not keen on paper coverings because paper can only ever be two-dimensional; they are concerned that it lacks the depth and relief of moulded plastic sheet and,

of course, you cannot paint it in your chosen colour. This may well be true in the larger scales such as O gauge and above, but in the smaller scales it is hard to discern the subtle relief of the mortar lines between courses of bricks from normal viewing distance.

The basic shape of the retaining wall can be made from stout card. You do not need to invest in expensive quality artist's card; in fact, if you look around it is easy to find card for free, such as the backing card used for notepads. Cereal packets are free and plentiful, but the card is too thin. Corrugated cardboard is usually free and easy to cut for its thickness; however, the corrugations do not provide a flat surface for applying brick paper (plastic sheet would be fine).

A simple retaining wall with basic arches and pillars is easy to construct by laminating successive layers of card and brick paper. Start with the rearmost layer to get the overall shape and size of the wall. This is just a simple rectangle and it is easy enough to attach the brick paper. Many different glues are suitable, though ones for card and paper are the best. Apply the glue thinly and evenly, otherwise lumps and bumps will become apparent. Some brick papers are quite thin and excessive glue can soak through the brick paper and spoil it.

A simple hassle-free way to attach the brick paper is to use strips of double-sided sticky tape. This is not the industrial-strength stuff beloved of *Blue Peter*, but the much thinner tape used by greetings card makers. The layer of glue that it leaves behind is very fine and will not show even with very thin brick papers.

Whatever glue you use, and no matter how thick your card, be aware that as the glue dries it may cause the card to bow inwards. To prevent this happening, leave the brick paper and card to dry thoroughly overnight weighted under a couple of heavy hardback books.

You can use the first piece of the wall as a template to cut out the next piece, which will be for the arches. Then draw on the arches and pillars. The size of the arches and where you put them are a matter of personal taste; look through books on real railways for inspiration. The half-circle of the arch can be drawn using a suitably sized tin as a template.

The waste material between the arches can be cut out. Use a sharp knife and a steel-edged ruler. As the card may be quite thick, make several passes with the knife to cut through rather than trying to do it all in one go. The arch is a little bit harder; if you remove the waste up to the bottom of the arch you may be able to cut it out with scissors (an old pair of nail scissors is perfect for this). Alternatively, use a craft knife to cut the arch freehand, or, if you are uncertain about being accurate, use the base of a suitably sized tin.

Now cover the resulting arches and pillars with brick paper and once more leave to dry weighted under books. Use one complete piece of brick paper; once the glue is dry, you can cut out the waste. Cut the paper a couple of millimetres from the card, then fold the paper around the edge of the card and glue it to the back of the card. This results in a pleasing three-dimensional effect. Once again, the arch is a little tricky, but by making a series of small cuts, the paper can be folded under the arch. It will leave gaps, but you are unlikely to be able to see under the arch.

The completed arches and pillars layer can now be glued to the rear layer. This completes the retaining wall, although you can make the pillars even thicker by adding more pieces to the front of them. Many walls were finished off with coping stones and these can be added with a thin strip of card notched every couple of millimetres to represent the gaps between the stones using nothing more than a sharp pencil.

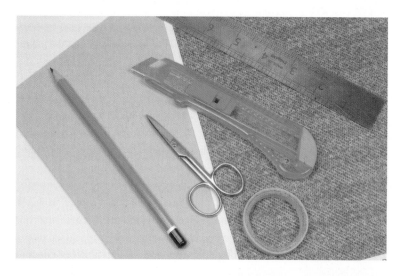

Retaining walls can be scratch-built using just a handful of basic modelling tools, some scrap cardboard, double-sided sticky tape and brick paper. The advantages are that you can build a large or long wall for next to nothing, to your chosen architectural style, and as a perfect fit into the space available on the layout.

The first step is to attach a piece of brick paper to some stout cardboard (at least 2mm thick). Double-sided sticky tape is quick and avoids any unsightly 'bubbles' from using a glue that has to be pasted on. Alternatively, as here, you can use one of the increasing range of brick papers with a self-adhesive backing. Leave the glue to dry overnight under a weight such as a pile of books, then cut to the required shape using the brick courses as a guide for getting it level and square.

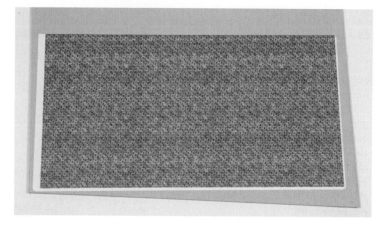

The resulting wall section will form the rear of the retaining wall, which will itself be made up from a series of laminations of wall sections. Use this rear section as a template to mark out the piece of cardboard that will be used for the front section.

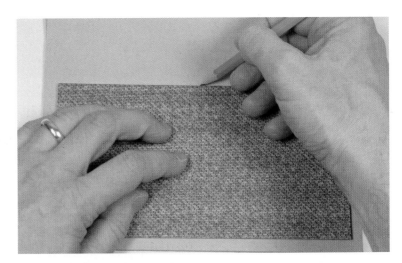

LEFT: *Use a pencil and a ruler to mark out where the supporting pillars will go, then draw in the supporting arches between the pillars. The base of a suitably sized tin (paint, beans, or whatever) provides a simple template for the arches. These arches can be full semicircles or shallower arcs; the design is entirely up to you.*

Cut out the rectangular portion of the front section that is between the pillars and below the arch. These straight cuts are simple to achieve with a steel ruler and will make it easier to cut out the arch. Note that cheap 'snap-off blade' knives are ideal for cutting thick card as you can regularly snap off the blade in order to ensure that the knife stays sharp. Thick cardboard soon dulls a blade and this can lead to inaccuracy and even accidents.

The arches are a little trickier to cut out. You can use your chosen template tin or carefully and slowly cut them freehand, as shown here. Note the use of a proper craft knife with a long, thin pointed blade, as this makes it easier to cut the arc of the arch.

RIGHT: To help cut the arch into the thicker cardboard, use a pair of small scissors to cut the waste cardboard up to the line of the arc. The resulting waste pieces can be flexed backwards slightly, which opens the curf formed by the initial cutting with the knife. This helps to cut the remainder of the depth of the arc accurately.

With all the waste material removed from the front section, place it over a piece of brick paper. Draw rough lines inside the shape of the pillars and arches, then cut out the waste material inside the drawn shape. Now glue the section to the rear of the resulting piece of brick paper.

Turn the front section over and cut a line in the back of the brick paper from the top of the pillar (where it meets the arc). Then fold the brick paper around the edge and rear of the pillar. Run your fingernail along each edge before you attempt to fold the brick paper in order to form neat folds along the edge of the cardboard.

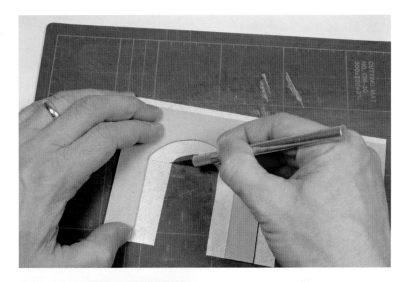

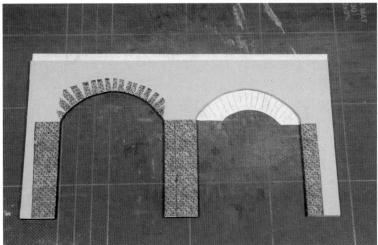

LEFT: *Cut a series of narrow strips into the rear of the brick paper under the arch mimicking the spokes of a wheel (seen on the right). These cuts can be done freehand, as geometric accuracy is not necessary. Then carefully fold the pieces of brick paper under the arch and secure them behind the section (seen on the left). Although the underneath of the arch may not be visible from all angles, a little work on this step will ensure a perfect finish.*

Finally, glue the front and rear sections together to complete the retaining wall. A small excess of brick paper was left at the top of the front section. This can be folded over the top of the laminated sections and secured behind the rear section to complete the top of the wall. Alternatively, coping stones can be made from a strip of card.

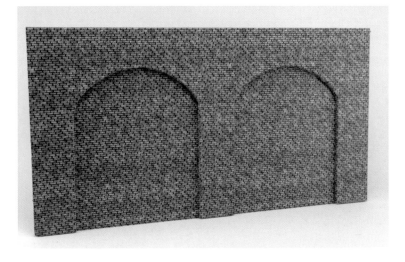

For long retaining walls, there is a limit to the length of a sheet of brick paper, usually no more than A4-sized. This means that adjacent sections need to be pieced together. To avoid an unsightly and visible join, make additional pillar sections that can be glued over the gap.

As well as being useful for covering the gap between adjacent sections, an additional layer of pillars can greatly enhance the three-dimensional appearance of a retaining wall. By scratch-building, you can make the wall as visually and architecturally stimulating as you want. This close-up view shows that with just three layers, a retaining wall made from nothing more than cardboard and brick paper looks just as good as much more expensive commercial offerings.

CHAPTER THREE

CROSSING THE RAILWAY

With the railway companies having so carefully marked out and protected their boundaries and thus defined the lineside, the next step was to allow a means for crossing the railway tracks for those people (and animals) with a genuine need to do so. As railways are long, thin things, it is not possible to walk around them; there has to be a means of getting across the tracks as safely as possible.

The most obvious method of crossing the railway is by means of a bridge over the railway (or by having the railway cross over the road so that you go under the tracks). Bridges, and to some extent tunnels, are part of the heavy engineering used to build the railways and not part of the lineside *per se*.

The next most obvious means of crossing the tracks is that most railway-like of devices, the level crossing. Next in the pecking order is the unguarded crossing (often a farm crossing), in its simplest form a barrow crossing for foot traffic only. With today's modern high-speed railway, the latter method is simply not safe enough and so footbridges have replaced simple ground level crossings.

Many preserved railways offer the chance still to see classic level crossing gates in action, such as at Ramsbottom Station on the East Lancashire Railway. The four gates are operated from a large wheel that is just visible in the window of the signal box. Although the gates are authentically preserved, the level crossing has still been modernized; note the macadam road surface instead of wooden planks, double white lines (no overtaking) and traffic lights to stop the road traffic.

This view of a modern level crossing at Hoscar is full of small details for the modeller. The barriers cover both sides of the road and have a gate that comes down beneath them. The barrier mechanisms are guarded by wire mesh screens for safety and there is a proliferation of signage. Note the relay cabinet far left, the palisade fencing and the emergency telephone on the post of the right-hand warning lights. The patchwork road surface with yellow and white markings is interesting, not least because of the small ramp to take the road up to rail level. *STUART BARDSLEY*

LEVEL CROSSINGS

There is something obviously railway-like about a level crossing. It is one of those things you immediately think about when looking at a railway. They would be found where the expense of a bridge could not be justified for the amount of traffic that needed to cross the railway at that point. While the traditional gates have given way to barriers and flashing signs, a level crossing is fundamentally the same today as it was over a hundred years ago.

A model of a level crossing has been a popular feature with modellers for many years; at one time they would often be included in train sets. It provides an interesting feature whereby the scenery can intersect the railway, or, rather, the roadway as a scenic element can cross over the tracks, thus joining one side of the lineside to the other. Level crossings are not just limited to stations; they are very often in the middle of nowhere. Most roadways came before the railways, so the latter has actually crossed the former.

LEVEL CROSSING KITS

The old Modelmaster OO gauge plastic kit for a level crossing is still going strong, now produced and sold by Dapol. It is a sturdy design that will make a single-track crossing; extra parts are included, such that two kits can be made to cross a double track. As usual with these kits, everything is moulded in battleship grey, so it is left to the modeller to paint the kit. Detail is basic; for example, there are no metal brackets moulded on the wooden gates, but a coat of white paint will soon produce an acceptable model. The roadway is modelled, including a ramp up to the rail level of the crossing. This is perhaps a little toy-like and unrealistic, but it makes for very easy installation on a layout.

The OO gauge level crossing kit produced by Dapol can be built as a single-track crossing. It has everything that you need, including ramps to bring the road up and over the railway tracks. Two kits can be used together to cross a double track by placing the ramps side by side and covering two of the holes for gateposts with blanks. The large piece for inserting between the two tracks (seen top left) can be cut to size depending on the distance from one track to the other.

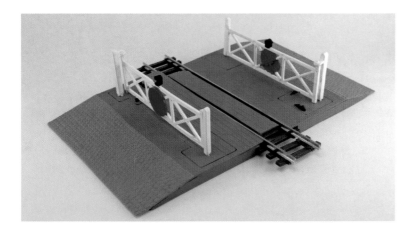

This is the Dapol level crossing kit made up to cross a single track with just one gate on each side. With careful construction and painting, the gates can actually be moved by hand. Note how the track is slightly elevated; the kit was designed assuming the use of foam ballast under the track. If the track is laid directly on to the baseboard, the level crossing can be lowered slightly by removing the side pieces and cutting off some of the approach ramp.

A very similar kit is offered in N gauge by Ratio Plastic Models. Despite the smaller scale, the level of detail is superior, including metal brackets on the wooden gates. Not only that, the parts are moulded in relevant colours (white for the gates and brown for the decking). Once again, ramps are included to bring the roadway up to rail height from the top of the baseboard. The kit will only make a crossing suitable for a double track, although the centre section could be omitted if only a single track needs to be crossed.

With both the Ratio Plastic Models and Dapol kits, do check that the inset pieces for the decking between the rails allow adequate clearance for the flanges on rolling stock wheels. Otherwise, this may lead to derailments. Check a selection of rolling stock from different manufacturers and even different types of models from the same manufacturers to ensure that there is sufficient clearance. If things are a bit tight or there are derailments, simply run the edges of the decking pieces over a sheet of wet & dry sandpaper. A couple of passes are all that is really needed and then refit and check again.

If the ramps on these kits are not to your liking, you can build up the roadway on the approach to the level crossing with card. The ramps themselves can be cut off and any gaps made good with a filler; a grab adhesive in the 'nails are not required' range is ideal.

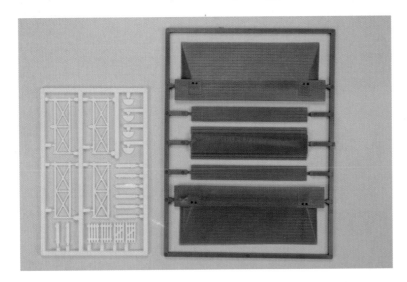

Ratio Plastic Models make kits for steam era level crossings in both OO gauge and N gauge, with the latter being illustrated here. The plastic parts are made in sympathetic colours (just the centre target needs to be painted red), although a coat of matt varnish would further improve this. The kit is designed to span a double track with double gates each side, although it could be used on a single track if required.

By far the biggest range of level crossing kits comes from Peco, with examples in all three of the major scales, namely O gauge, OO gauge and N gauge. Most are steam era gated crossings, but the OO gauge and N gauge ranges include the more modern lifting barrier type with (non-working) flashing lights.

The Peco N gauge sectional track range includes a single-track level crossing, which is supplied as integral to a piece of straight sectional track. This can be extended with an add-on piece to make a double-track level crossing. Even if not using sectional track, the fact that this crossing is available with the decking already installed means that it might be worth

ABOVE LEFT: The level crossing kits from Peco consist only of gates, so it is necessary for the modeller to build up the actual road crossing. Having laid the track, the first step is to add a layer of thick card on either side. This needs to be the width of the road and also the same depth as the sleepers (in this case N gauge). If necessary, use several layers of card to achieve the required depth.

ABOVE RIGHT: Add a layer of thinner card which is the same thickness as the moulded chairs that hold the rails to the sleepers. Butt this up to the chairs. This example has a road that is at a perfect right angle to the railway line. This was quite common, as even real railways find it easier to build a level crossing like this. If necessary, it is not much harder to have the road at an angle.

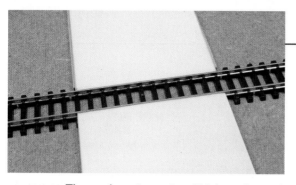 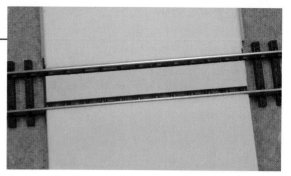

ABOVE LEFT: The top layer is a strip of 20thou plastic sheet, although a similar thickness of card would do just as well. This butts up against the web of the rail, in other words just below the top of the I-section of the rail. This ensures that the top of the rail is fractionally higher than the road surface; if they were the same height, there would be a risk of the road surface lifting the wheels of the rolling stock. For a locomotive, this would break the electrical connection, causing it to stall.

ABOVE RIGHT: To fill the gap between the rails, start with a piece of the thin card that is the same depth as the moulded chairs. Cut it to a width that will sit between the chairs.

ABOVE LEFT: The road surface once again utilizes 20thou plastic sheet. Its width is a case of trial and error. Start with a piece that fits between the rails with a gap of about 1mm either side. It is then important to try numerous different locomotives and rolling stock to check that the clearance is correct. If there is any hint of interference, cut a sliver off the side of the plastic (or rub it over a piece of sandpaper). Repeat this process until all wheels will pass over the level crossing without any problems.

ABOVE RIGHT: Use the same lamination of card and plastic sheet to build up the foundations at the sides for the gates, or, as in this case, just one each side for modern barriers. Note also how filler has been used to smooth the edge of the road and foundations since these are higher than the top of the baseboard.

The road surface is painted dark grey (not black) and white lines added using a paint pen and ruler. The type of road marking (dashed lines, solid lines, double lines, yellow hatching and so on) varies depending on location and era, so check photographs pertinent to what you are modelling. Ballasting and scenic ground cover disguise the height difference between the road and the baseboard.

considering if you are unsure about adding the decking. The sectional track is easily joined to flexible track using Peco's own rail-joiners.

None of the other Peco level crossing kits comes with any kind of decking, so there is an element of scratch-building required to complete them. Steam era crossings usually had a timber decking of pieces running parallel with the rails. These are easily replicated using planked plastic sheet, such as that produced by Slater's Plastikard, or by scribing plain plastic sheet yourself. The earlier comments about checking for clearance for wheel flanges apply equally to this.

It is best to set the decking about 0.5mm below the height of the top of the rail. There is always a slight 'bump' as you go across a real level crossing, but of course in real life the clearances are much finer. It is important to make sure that the deck of the crossing is just below rail height to avoid the risk of lifting rolling stock wheels. This would lead to stalling of locomotives, as they would be effectively isolated from the power in the track.

The same approach applies for the modern era, where the macadam road surface is now filled between the rails. Plastic sheet or even card can be used and things are a little simpler since no planking needs to be scribed on.

SCRATCH-BUILT LEVEL CROSSINGS

Barrier level crossings can be any width and cross as many tracks as you like, since there are no gates to close across the track, only barriers to protect the road. Steam era gates would close together, whether protecting the road or the railway. Modellers tend to build level crossings at a perfect right angle to the track, but this was not always the case. There were many examples of complicated crossings involving acute angles and multiple tracks or roads. In such cases, the gates supplied in level crossing kits will not be suitable.

Scratch-building crossing gates is not as easy as it looks. Although such gates used fairly hefty timbers, these are going to be quite thin once they are scaled down for a model. There is a risk that the gate will be flimsy and prone to damage, especially if you want it actually to work.

The best material to use is brass, with pieces soldered together for strength. A template with pins inserted as guides will help to keep everything straight, but this really is something for the advanced modeller. It is all too easy accidentally to unsolder a join while soldering another on something so flimsy.

Plastic strip is available as square section, which is ideal. This will be easier to work with as it is simple to cut with a knife and only requires a liquid polystyrene glue to put it together. Fitting the cross-bracing pieces can be rather fiddly. The result will look more than acceptable, but it could be quite a fragile model.

A better solution might be to combine the gates from several kits. This is quite easy to do, as the moulded plastic pieces are already quite strong. Some

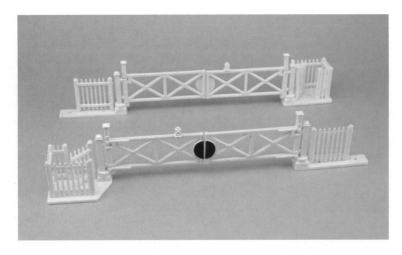

Peco makes a kit for a traditional gated level crossing in OO gauge (shown here) and N gauge that is simple to construct. The red target in the middle is pre-painted, though the kit can be further enhanced by painting the lamps and picking out the ironwork in black using a fine paintbrush. Only the gates are supplied, so it is up to the modeller to install the actual crossing. Note the wicket gate for pedestrian crossing, although as the kit parts are handed, they do not actually line up with each other.

kits like those from Peco have the red target moulded (and painted) into the gate, while the kits from Dapol and Ratio Plastic Models do not. Level crossing gates only had one target in the middle, so this would have to be taken into account.

CROSSING KEEPER'S COTTAGES

Level crossings at stations and junctions were controlled by the signal box. Out in the countryside in the middle of nowhere, there would not have been a signal box, but the railways still had to employ someone to open and close the gates in conjunction with the railway traffic. A small hut might have been provided for the crossing keeper and many of the models available for platelayers' huts would be suitable. More common was to provide permanent accommodation for the crossing keeper in the form of a cottage or small house.

This level crossing on the line from Wigan Wallgate to Southport is a mix of old and nearly new. Dominating the scene is the house that would originally have been used by the crossing keeper (note the ground level bay window for visibility up and down the line). The modern barriers do not have the latest dropdown gates, nor do they fully block the road. The old-style fencing and wicket gates are straight out of the steam era, yet they are still going strong to this day. STUART BARDSLEY

Kestrel Designs makes a model of a crossing keeper's cottage in N gauge. This is a plastic kit for a small single-storey dwelling. Some rudimentary crossing gates are also included, but the model is probably best used in conjunction with the Ratio Plastic Models or Peco kits. In OO gauge, Dornaplas makes a kit specifically marketed as a crossing keeper's cottage, as does Wills.

Houses and cottages come in a variety of shapes and sizes and there were no set designs for crossing keepers' accommodation. Therefore, you could scratch-build a small cottage, or use an available model for a house, such as one of the card kits from Metcalfe Models.

UNGUARDED CROSSINGS

Any public highway would have been protected by crossing gates, but there were (and indeed still are) instances of other crossings that were not protected. These were usually where a farm track crossed the line. It was beholden to the farmer to 'stop, look and listen' before crossing the line.

These unguarded or 'ungated' crossings would have looked like a level crossing with timbers to

Kestrel Designs in N gauge offers a model that is specifically marketed as a 'crossing keeper's cottage'; however, any modest dwelling could serve as a home for a crossing keeper in whatever scale you model. This kit builds into a nice compact model and a couple of basic level crossing gates are included.

cross the line, but without crossing gates. An adjacent field might have been gated, especially if there was livestock in it, but this is quite different to a level crossing gate.

Modelling an unguarded crossing is really just a case of building a narrow level crossing without the traditional railway infrastructure of gates. Sometimes the crossing might have just been a footpath or right of way, and these may have been protected by a wicket gate; Peco includes these in its level crossing kits and as a separate item.

If making your own crossing timbers does not appeal, there are kits for barrow crossings in OO gauge from Ten Commandments and Ratio Plastic Models. Barrow crossings are a piece of steam era infrastructure that were just a wooden deck between the rails that allowed a porter's barrow to be wheeled from one platform to another. Although barrow crossings were found in stations, there is no reason why these kits cannot be used elsewhere to represent an unguarded crossing.

FOOTBRIDGES

While it was quite acceptable to have unguarded crossings in the steam era, it is certainly not the case in the modern era, where safety concerns are much greater. This is with good reason; trains are a lot faster these days and actually a lot quieter without the 'chuff chuff' of a steam locomotive's exhaust. Many lines have now been electrified and either a third rail or overhead wires pose additional hazards.

Since there are still many rights of way crossing railway lines, a safe means of allowing people to cross them is a must and there is no simpler way than a footbridge. These modern structures are built from steel sections, which are practical though lacking in any architectural merit compared to the station footbridges of the steam era.

The box-like structure of these steel footbridges would be quite simple to scratch-build from either plastic sheet or card. The framing is easily added from plastic strip, or strips can be cut from card. The steps may be a bit of a challenge.

The relevant size of square plastic strip can be cut into steps that can be glued together to form the stairway. If this proves to be too fiddly, another option is to use the steps from another bridge kit (for a steam era footbridge), although this is a little wasteful as the majority of the kit is discarded.

There is a kit for a modern steel footbridge in N gauge from Kestrel Designs. This has pre-coloured pieces so painting is not absolutely essential, although it will dramatically improve the final appearance of the model.

Another option, for both OO gauge and N gauge, is the Ratio Plastic Models kit for a concrete footbridge. Concrete was used to make all sorts of lineside structures, particularly by the Southern Railway, and these kits come moulded in a suitable colour to mimic concrete. Such footbridges are modular by nature so they resemble the modern steel footbridges. With the relevant coat of paint, they can be made to look like steel structures.

One problem with using footbridge kits is that they are intended to be platform-mounted. A footbridge in the middle of nowhere to take a right of way across the railway would not be on a platform. Therefore, it is necessary in some way to make up the missing height of the platform. If the model railway represents an electrified line with overhead wires, it may be necessary to add further height to the footbridge to clear the wires.

The first option is to create an artificial platform by modelling some landform underneath the bridge that is about as high as a platform. Since the height of a platform is a relatively small proportion of the overall height of a footbridge, a modest amount of scenery in terms of a very shallow hill is easily accommodated underneath the bridge.

A second option is to utilize two kits, using parts from one to extend the steps of another. This would use most of the parts from the second kit, which minimizes the amount of waste. Simply joining two sets of stairways may make the bridge too high, even to clear overhead wires, but it is simple enough to cut down one set of the steps to the required height for the footbridge.

There are some very good footbridge kits available in OO gauge and N gauge, but they are designed to be installed on a platform, which therefore raises them up. This Kestrel N-gauge footbridge just about gives clearance for a locomotive when it is simply placed on the baseboard surface.

Adding a thick piece of cardboard under the footbridge raises it slightly, but this is enough to give a more realistic-looking level of clearance over the locomotive. For a modern bridge like the Kestrel kit, the cardboard looks like a concrete foundation. Alternatively, it could be hidden under scenic scatter materials.

CHAPTER FOUR

LINESIDE STRUCTURES

If you take a railway journey today, you might see one or two buildings that are a part of the railway, excluding the obvious station-related ones. Step back in time to the steam era and you would have seen more structures at the side of the railway. Most of these structures would have been fairly small, such as platelayers' huts. They would have been quite commonplace, yet quite varied. The biggest structure would likely have been a signal box or a water tower.

PLATELAYERS' HUTS

It is hard to appreciate in this age of big yellow track machines just how labour-intensive the maintenance of railway tracks once was. Modern track machines do all the lifting, packing and tamping in one go, either on new track or old. In the steam era, all of this hard work was done by hand. Track gangs of 'plate-layers' (possibly a reference to the earliest cast-iron rails that were more like plates) would be allocated a stretch of line and it was their responsibility to check it for safety and to keep it maintained. Pride in the job was intense and awards were made for the best-maintained lengths of track.

The localized nature of this work meant that the track gangs needed a base location on their patch of the line. The railway companies provided a simple hut in which they could store their tools, shelter from the elements and, most importantly, make a cup of tea. Most of these dwellings were modest affairs, but their sheer variety means a wide choice for the modeller in terms of what is available as products from the model railway manufacturers. While the hut is very much symbolic of the steam era, a few can still be found quietly rotting away on the modern railway; often they were built so well that they have certainly stood the test of time.

Platelayers' huts were made from many different materials. Simple wooden structures were cheap and quick to build, though even these may have been provided with a brick chimney. Stone-built huts were often made from locally available stone, a bit like the stone walling used to define the boundary. Perhaps the best-built huts were those made from brick, miniature houses with all the durability of brick walls and a tiled roof. Concrete huts were also quite common, the ability to prefabricate the walls and roof from concrete panels making them cheap and quick to build, as well as versatile (they could be made small or large thanks to the standardization of the interconnecting parts).

KITS FOR PLATELAYERS' HUTS

While there are no ready-to-plant models for plate-layers' huts, the best starting point for a novice kit builder in OO gauge is the Peco hut. This is moulded in plastic and the basic four walls come as one complete part, so there is no need to worry about getting the walls straight and true. There are a few additional parts, such as the roof and a door, to complete the structure. If you have never made a kit before, this is an ideal kit on which to cut your teeth.

The Peco kit represents a wooden hut and it is moulded in black plastic. If you really want to keep things simple you could leave it unpainted, but plastic always looks like plastic, not wood. It is a simple matter to paint the walls a brown 'creosote' type colour and the roof a dark grey to represent a roofing material. The door would probably have been painted black or brown, although a mid to light grey helps the detail of the door to stand out a little.

Peco also supports the other main commercial gauges. It does an excellent pack for N gauge modellers that has three brick-built huts and two wooden huts. Two of the brick huts are moulded in

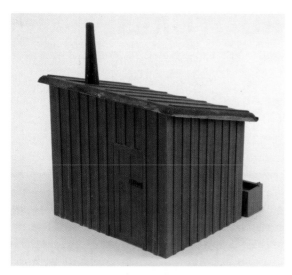

One of the simplest OO gauge platelayers' huts to make is the one from Peco representing a wooden construction with a sloping roof. The four walls are a one-piece moulding, with just the door and roof to fit, and details such as a stovepipe and a water trough. The black plastic needs painting and a brown colour followed by a wash of light grey really lifts this simple model.

This diminutive model in N gauge is by Peco and represents a typical wooden platelayers' hut with flat roof and brick chimney. It is a very easy kit to build, despite the small scale, consisting of just four walls, a base, a roof and the chimney. The superbly detailed figure is also by Peco and helps to create a more interesting scene than just a building on its own.

a reasonable 'brick colour' plastic, while the third is moulded in blue to represent engineers' blue brick. The so-called blue bricks were a tougher brick than you would find in a normal building, their extra strength being required for engineering structures like retaining walls, tunnels and bridges. Undoubtedly there would have been enough bricks going spare to build the odd platelayers' hut, so a blue structure would look a little different on any layout, though only where blue brick would have been used in quantity, such as near a tunnel.

Peco makes O gauge kits for platelayers' huts representing both brick and wooden varieties. The larger scale means that these kits are full of detail. While they are simple to build and contain few parts, those parts are highly detailed, such as the grain of the wood for the doors and the texture of the felt on the roof.

Ten Commandments produces a wide range of platelayers' huts in all three of the major modelling scales. These are generally one-piece plaster castings with very good detail. The solid castings

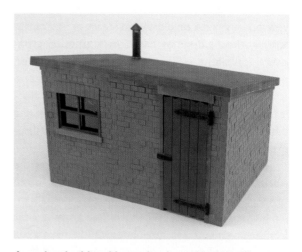

A modest building like a platelayers' hut is still quite an imposing structure in O gauge. The larger scale allows a high level of detail to be incorporated. This model has been constructed from the Peco plastic kit. Just a few parts are included (walls, roof, door, window and chimney), so this is an ideal project for anyone who wants to have a go at the larger scale. Once again, careful painting results in a superb model.

do mean that you cannot see through any windows, though the interiors would have been gloomy anyway; with careful painting, this is not obvious. Solid plaster is a little heavy, which could be an issue if you are building a portable layout, although the modest proportions of a small hut are unlikely to make a huge difference to the overall weight of your layout.

The slightly porous nature of the plaster opens up huge opportunities for getting some really good effects when painting these models. You can seal the plaster with an undercoat, then finish the models with any paint from enamels to acrylics. Alternatively, washes of acrylics diluted with water enable great tonal variation to be achieved, especially on the huts that represent wood as the construction material. Nothing in life is ever all one colour unless it is brand new; things like the weather and pollution take their toll and materials can stain or fade in differing degrees in different places.

The trick to applying washes to a plaster casting is to be patient and be prepared to paint the model two or even three times. It is the old adage that you can always apply more paint, but it cannot be removed if you add too much. Apply a first wash of paint, then leave the model to dry. Acrylics are very fast-drying; even with their high water content they should be

The small size of a platelayers' hut is practical for a solid plaster-cast model such as this wooden hut by Ten Commandments. The model is not too heavy for use on a portable layout. The solid-cast window has been painted black, representing a dark interior. The odd chip or bubble in the plaster casting lends character to the representation of a well-weathered wooden building.

dry within five minutes. Wait this long to see how the paint will appear when dry. It often looks a different shade when it is wet, so do not be tempted to add more paint immediately until you are sure what the final dry colour will be.

Ten Commandments makes a number of different plaster-cast platelayers' huts in all the major railway modelling scales. They are sold unpainted, such as this example of a wooden hut on a stone base. It is a simple matter to paint the model, a modest project that can be finished in one or two evenings.

The first step is to apply the main colour, a brown to represent faded creosoted timber. Whether using acrylics or enamels, thin the paint so that it is actually a wash. This will soak into the plaster at first and, in places, the colour of the plaster still shows through. This is a superb effect, as the tonal variation looks extremely realistic.

RIGHT: With the main part of the hut painted, use a small paintbrush to pick out the details such as the chimney pot, the door and the stone base. While the door would in reality be likely to have been painted the same colour as the walls, choosing a different colour helps it to stand out as a detail.

The roof of the hut is another area to receive a wash of paint, this time with black. Note the use of a broad flat brush; this helps to cover the area quickly without leaving any obvious brushstrokes. As the wash soaks into the plaster, being quick with the brushstokes helps to avoid getting too much paint on in one go. This allows the plaster colour to show through in places, making the roof look old and weathered.

As a solid plaster casting, the windows on the model are not transparent. The first step is to paint the window black; windows in buildings that are not illuminated tend to look dark in real life. The glazing bars can be picked out in white. If you have a steady hand with a paintbrush, you can paint this detail. A quicker and easier method is to use a 'paint pen', a sort of ballpoint pen that 'writes' in white.

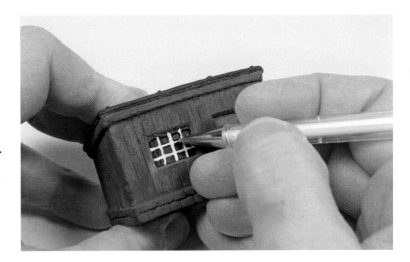

The model can be painted in just a few hours and the result is very convincing. Plaster-cast buildings can exhibit the odd chip; you can fill them in if you want, but they just add to the character of a building like this. The flexible rubber casting moulds can sometimes allow a bit of deviation from straight horizontals and verticals, but this adds even more character.

Acrylic paints are easy to water down, just like watercolour paints. Start with something like a fifty–fifty mix of paint and water, and paint different sections or patches of the building. Next, add more water to lighten the colour of the paint and paint other sections. Finally, add more water and paint the remaining sections. This gives different colours to the model. Even the amount of paint that is on the brush can affect the colour, as it soaks into the plaster differently.

After a few light coats of watered-down paint, the plaster will probably start to seal. By this time, the base colour should be complete and the model can be finished off with a very dilute wash of black or brown to give the structure a weathered feel.

The plaster is, of course, a very good representation of the mortar used in a brick wall. Use a broad, flat brush to apply a brick or stone colour; dragging the brush across the model at a very low angle will prevent too much paint getting into the mortar

Some platelayers' huts were quite distinctive to the railway company that built them, particularly the sectional cast-concrete huts built by the Southern Railway and this example from the LNER. The OO gauge model shown here is a plaster kit from Ten Commandments; all that is required is to paint it and glue on the roof.

courses, creating a pleasing representation of the mortar.

For something slightly different, Ten Commandments produces a range of concrete huts in all the major scales. These models are based on a London

and North Eastern Railway (LNER) design, though they are similar to designs used by other companies. The modular design of these buildings means that Ten Commandments offers small or medium versions of the huts. Roxey Mouldings makes a white-metal kit for a small version of this type of hut, as well as Southern Railway ones.

Another of the old Kitmaster mouldings offered by Dapol in OO gauge is the assorted trackside models kit. This includes a flat-roofed wooden platelayers' hut that is simple to construct and makes a very typical example of the wooden hut. The second structure in the kit is advertised as a coal merchant's office, being a wooden hut with a pitched slate roof; however, there is no reason why this small hut cannot be used as a platelayers' hut. Remember that they came in all shapes and sizes, so it is worth looking around at kits containing different structures to see what can be adapted.

Another good example of this adaptability is the yard office kit offered in OO gauge by Ratio Plastic Models. This single-sprue kit offers all the parts needed to make a small brick-built structure with a pitched tiled roof. The quality of the moulding and the fit of the parts are as expected from this manufacturer, so this makes another good kit for the beginner. The finished model looks just as good as a platelayers' hut, as it does as a yard office.

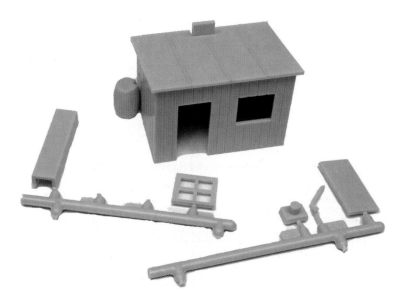

The old Kitmaster OO gauge plastic kit for a wooden platelayers' hut is now produced by Dapol, but even after fifty years this is still an effective little model. This view shows the walls constructed and the test-fitting of the roof. Note how the other parts have been left on the sprues; this makes it easier to paint them before adding them to the model, especially the smaller parts.

The flat plastic roof in the kit is a bit too smooth to represent a real roof, which would likely be asphalt strips or tarred with chippings on top. To add a little texture before painting, a sheet of toilet paper is glued on to the roof. Simply flood the paper with liquid polystyrene cement and it will weld itself to the plastic. This does produce a lot of fumes, so make sure that you do this in a well-ventilated area.

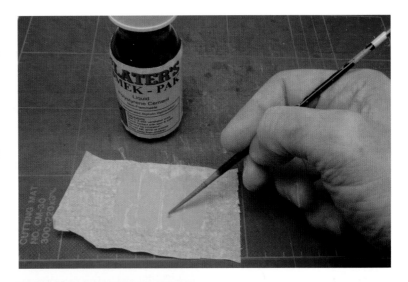

LEFT: An advantage of the liquid polystyrene glue is that it sets very quickly. The roof is turned over and then a sharp craft knife is used to trim off the excess paper. The roof piece is a very thick moulding, so there is no danger of it warping as a result of being flooded with the liquid glue.

The roof has now been painted with a wash of black paint. An enamel paint was used, diluted with thinners (alternatively, use acrylic paint or watercolours diluted with water). The thin wash gives tonal variation and avoids one perfect overall colour, which would be unrealistic. Similarly, the walls have received a dirty brown colour, then a wash of light grey in order to make the model much more interesting.

Ratio Plastic Models makes a plastic kit in OO gauge for a 'coal merchant's office'. Do not be put off by this description of the model, as it is perfectly suited to being a platelayers' hut. All the parts come on one sprue and this is a simple kit to build. The only tools needed are a craft knife, some tweezers and a bit of wet & dry sandpaper to remove any rough edges where the parts were separated from the sprue. A liquid polystyrene glue is best for construction, applied to joints with a small paintbrush.

RIGHT: It is important to get the corners between two wall pieces as square as possible. This means that the mitred-corner joints will then be virtually invisible, as well as ensuring that other parts (such as the roof) will also be a good fit. The inexpensive tool shown here consists of two square pieces (an inner and an outer) with magnets to hold the two model parts together. Note the cut-out in the corner of the tool to allow glue to be applied without getting it stuck to the tool itself.

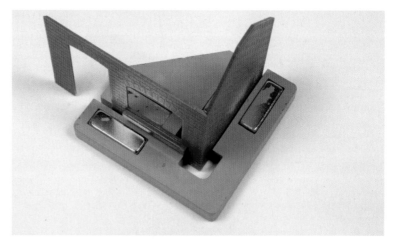

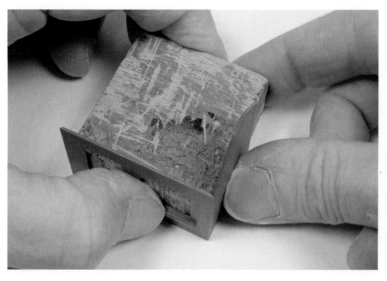

Although the two-part holding tool is quite inexpensive, all that is really needed for square corners is a block of wood against which to hold the plastic parts. Use a piece of hardwood if possible as it is more durable and cut it on a compound mitre saw, as this ensures perfectly square edges. As can be seen, you do need both hands to hold the parts. Liquid polystyrene glue does set very quickly, so the parts only need to be held for a few seconds. Then leave the joints for a few minutes to harden fully before further handling.

By joining end and side walls to form L-shapes, the basic structure of the model holds itself upright. It is then a simple matter to bring the two L-shapes together on a flat surface to glue the remaining two corners together. The result is the main shell of the building, which will be sufficiently robust for handling while the remaining parts are attached.

LEFT: The model is now ready for painting. Note that some parts (ridge tiles, door, window and chimney pot) have been left off, as they will be easier to paint separately. The roof might have been easier to leave off for painting, but it needs to be in place for the gutters and downspouts to be attached. It is simpler to glue the latter on at this stage, rather than after they have been painted.

Painting starts with the overall base colours, such as red for the bricks and grey for the roof slates. It is always best to paint plastic, even if it is originally the correct colour. Once the base colours have dried, the details such as the window sill and the downspouts can be painted with a fine brush.

The completed model would look superb by the lineside of any steam era layout. Any small brick building such as this coal merchant's office, a yard office or a weighbridge building will look authentic as a platelayers' hut. Such buildings could still be used on more up-to-date layouts, although they would be in a more derelict state; this could be achieved by omitting the window and doors, and possibly having the gutters hanging off at one end.

Kestrel Designs offers a coal office in N gauge that could easily be a platelayers' hut, just like the one from Ratio Plastic Models. These simple plastic kits are easy to assemble, even allowing for the smaller scale of N gauge. If you think that N gauge is too small for kit-building, this could be an ideal starting point to convince you otherwise. Kestrel Designs also makes a kit for a pair of yard huts that could similarly be used as platelayers' huts.

SCRATCH-BUILT HUTS

If you are an accomplished kit-builder but you are looking to have a go at scratch-building a structure of some kind, a platelayers' hut is about as simple a structure as you are likely to find. The easiest option is to build a wooden hut, not least because they tended to have a flat roof rather than a pitched one.

Wooden planks are easy to represent. You can simply build the structure out of card and the lines between the planks can be made by scoring the card with nothing more complicated than a pencil. Use card that is at least 1mm thick and a harder pencil

such as a 2H, since these will score a deeper groove than a softer leaded pencil.

Plastic card is a good material for scratch-building, as the parts can be welded together using a liquid polystyrene glue. It is a little harder to cut than a paper-based card, but the trick is to make several passes with a sharp knife until the plastic is cut through. A pencil will not score plastic, while a knife only cuts very thin lines rather than grooves. A metal scribe, as used to mark sheet metal, is an ideal tool, as it leaves a groove. Another option is an Olfa cutter, which has a blade that gouges rather than cuts; a few light passes with one of these tools will leave a very neat groove.

A doorway is quite easy to cut out of the plastic. Cut down the two sides of the doorway, then partially cut the top of the door. It is then possible to snap the plastic offcut away from the wall. Windows are a little trickier, since all the lines to be cut are internal (that is, none go to the edge of the plastic). The trick here is also to cut the diagonals between the corners; the resulting triangles are easier to snap off. It may

This is another very small N-gauge model, a simple plastic kit by Kestrel Designs. It is sold as a 'coal office', but the basic design makes it just as appropriate as a platelayers' hut. Despite being moulded in suitable colours, all the parts have been painted to avoid the shiny look of plastic. The one slight exception to this is the roof; it is the original plastic colour, but it has received a coat of matt varnish to stop it looking shiny.

also help to drill a large hole in the middle of the window aperture to help snap off the waste material.

A brick-built structure is not much more difficult to make than a wooden one, though there is the added complication of 'bricks'. Wills makes brick sheets from plastic sheet that is thick enough for a model; however, joining the pieces at the corners requires care and the usual approach is to use sandpaper to form a mitre on the two faces to be joined.

An alternative is to use plain plastic (or even paper-based card) to build a shell to which can be applied either a brick paper, or the thin brick-embossed plastic sheet produced by Slater's Plastikard. The former may be easier, as it offers the possibility of wrapping a single sheet all the way around the structure, thus avoiding any unsightly joins.

Flat roofs are very easy to make as they are just a simple rectangle. They can be painted grey, but one option is to use a piece of wet & dry sandpaper. This fine-grade sandpaper looks like the type of felt roof that would have been used, though remember to give it a wash of weathering paint to make it look like it has been rained on for many years.

A tiled roof is really just two rectangles, which is not much more difficult than a flat roof. The tiles themselves can be represented with paper sheets from the likes of Metcalfe Models or Superquick Model Kits, though bear in mind that most layouts are viewed from above, so, unlike real life, we tend to see more of the roof than the walls. Ratio Plastic Models and Wills make sheets of tiles, though these can be a bit thick. Best of all is the embossed-tile plastic sheet from Slater's Plastikard.

Many platelayers' huts had a brick chimney, even if the rest of the structure was wood, since everything in the steam era was coal-powered. A chimney can be made just like the walls, though the much narrower profile can be more challenging. A simpler option is to imagine that the hut just has a stove since all this requires is a tube to take the fumes out through the roof and a tube is easily represented with anything from a piece of wire to a drinking straw.

FOGMEN'S HUTS

If you have ever driven a car through thick fog you will know how hard it is to see where you are. While modern train drivers have automatic warning systems and train protection, it still requires extreme professionalism. Imagine, then, the steam era and trying to take several hundred tons of train through thick fog without all those modern safety systems.

Trains run to timetables and slowing things to a stop with fog causes timetable chaos. More importantly, safety is the railway's number one concern, as several terrible accidents have been caused by fog.

During the steam era, in times of fog it fell to the fogman to help the railway to run safely, even to run at all. These men were usually trackworkers drafted in at a moment's notice. They were positioned at important places such as near signals and their job was to warn train drivers where they were, either with bright lamps or by putting detonators on the line (these are small explosives that detonate when a train runs over them, a clearly audible warning to the driver).

The prospect of standing around on a cold, damp and foggy night cannot have been too exciting. Most railway companies provided some form of shelter for the fogman and a place to store lamps and detonators. These little huts make for interesting models on our miniature railways (even if we will never be plagued by any kind of actual fog).

MODELS OF FOGMEN'S HUTS

For many decades, the old OO gauge Merit fogman and hut must have graced hundreds of layouts. Thankfully, this set is still available from Model Scene Accessories. The hut is a basic open-fronted affair in black plastic that would be easily enhanced by a lick of paint to remove the plastic finish. The brazier to keep the fogman warm has a nice representation of glowing coals. The fogman carrying a lamp himself is a good model, in his thick grey overcoat and wearing a red scarf. These three parts are ready to plant on your layout, though be wary of having a heavily dressed gentleman if your model railway is set in high summer.

A very detailed plastic kit is available from Ratio Plastic Models to make a concrete hut with wooden doors. This kit has many delicate parts and fine detail, even down to a spade and fork and a grinding stone (details that could be used in front of a platelayers' hut).

Ten Commandments makes unpainted plaster-cast models of a classic fogman's hut with closed door in both OO gauge and O gauge. These castings just

The old Merit fogman, hut and brazier must have been used on countless layouts over the last fifty years or more. Thankfully, these well-detailed models are still available through Model Scene Accessories. As always, the plastic hut would benefit from a coat of brown paint and the figure needs a little bit of touching up here and there. The features on the figure are excellent, even by today's standards – the gentleman even has a drooping moustache.

require painting a suitable wood colour and installing on a layout. It is also worth noting that these small shed-like structures could easily represent an outside privy. Not all signal boxes had an integral toilet, especially the smaller ones, so a fogman's hut could be discreetly positioned near the signal box.

SCRATCH-BUILDING A FOGMAN'S HUT

A fogman's hut is really just a smaller version of a classic wooden platelayers' hut with a flat roof. It can easily be represented with scored card or plastic

ABOVE LEFT: Ratio Plastic Models produces an OO gauge kit for a very comfy-looking fogman's hut. It represents a precast concrete panel construction with wooden door and a substantial stove for those long, cold winter nights. With the doors closed, it is modelled as not being used. This is far more typical, since few of us operate our layouts with actual fog, preferring the idyll of a summer's day.

ABOVE RIGHT: This OO gauge plaster-cast fogman's hut from Ten Commandments is a simple structure with some lovely wood effect on the planking. The sides have been painted a basic 'creosote' colour; however, the roof has been left unpainted, as the natural tonal variation in the colour of the plaster gives a good weathered effect. This model is not just useful as a fogman's hut; many signal boxes did not have an integral lavatory so this could be placed close by for the signalman's convenience.

card. If the options for adding a plank effect to plastic card with a scriber or Olfa cutter are not practical on a much smaller structure, you can buy plank-effect plastic sheet from the likes of Slater's Plastikard and Evergreen Scale Models.

The simplest approach would be a hut with doors in the closed position like the Ten Commandments model. This makes it easier to form the hut shape, as some internal bracing can be added for strength. The greater strength offered by using plastic parts joined with a liquid polystyrene glue means that you could model an open-fronted hut like the one produced by Model Scene Accessories.

LAMP HUTS

Before the widespread use of electricity, semaphore signals required lamps to indicate the position of the signal after dark. These lamps were oil burners and they had to be changed every couple of days (this is the main reason that semaphore signals have a ladder). The men who changed the lamps needed a place for the safe storage of spare lamps, paraffin and tools. Thus the railway companies provided lamp huts, which were quite distinct from platelayers' huts.

Lamp huts were almost always constructed out of corrugated iron, since wood is not an ideal material

Wills makes a plastic kit for a classic lamp hut representing corrugated iron construction. Details include buckets for sand to be used in case the flammable contents of the hut catch fire and a couple of oil drums to complete the scene.

when storing flammable materials. They were often painted in railway company colours, such as the light and dark stone paints favoured by the GWR. While lamp huts were usually found in station areas, since this is where the largest concentrations of signals tended to be, they could be found by the lineside between stations, especially at junctions where, once again, there would be a large number of signals.

Ten Commandments produces plaster-cast models of a typical lamp hut in both OO gauge and O gauge. Wills makes a detailed plastic kit for a lamp hut. Both models can be painted for whichever railway company you are modelling.

Scratch-building is not impossible since model corrugated material is available, either thin corrugated metal, which is expensive, or corrugated plastic sheet. Some modellers 'roll their own' using a two-part press into which they put the thicker kind of foil to be found in takeaway meal cartons. Lamps huts tend to have a curved roof and this can be difficult to form whatever material you use without damaging the corrugations.

WATER TOWERS

Another of those intrinsically steam era pieces of infrastructure is the water tower. They tend to be associated with stations where a locomotive might fill up while waiting for passengers, though they could also be found in other locations. While water troughs do not need a train to stop to take on water, they still need to be refilled rapidly, for which a water tower was often provided. They might also be found at a passing loop where the locomotive could replenish its water supply while waiting for another train to overtake it.

There are ready-to-plant water towers from Bachmann Scenecraft and Hornby as well as a number of kits. Dapol provides a plastic kit in OO gauge for a tank that is on a metal framework rather than the more usual brick base, though these tended to be more common in locomotive depots. Superquick Model Kits provides a card kit in OO gauge, as does Metcalfe Models. In N gauge, Kestrel Designs provides a plastic kit.

Scratch-building a water tower to suit your own particular requirements is quite easy. All water towers require a tank and these are basically just a simple box structure with some framing. They can be made out of card or plastic card. While rivets would probably be a feature of the tank, this is a fine detail that can be omitted without the model looking particularly incorrect (you have to be very close to notice the absence or otherwise of rivets).

Some water tanks were covered, usually by planks of wood, but possibly by a metal cover (with a hatch at one corner for inspection). Either is simple to build and the wood can be represented by scoring card or plastic card, or buying planked plastic sheet such as that produced by Slater's Plastikard.

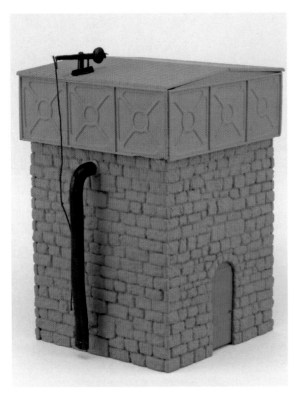 

ABOVE LEFT: *Water towers are not necessarily big buildings and a more modest affair would be found serving a branch line or narrow-gauge railway. Wills makes a simple-to-construct plastic kit for a modest-sized water tower with a covered cast-iron tank sitting atop a stone tower.*

ABOVE RIGHT: *Metcalfe Models makes an OO gauge card kit for a typical design of water tower. Such a building could be found anywhere that steam locomotives needed replenishing and not necessarily in a station. A passing loop would see trains stopped to allow faster trains to pass by and what better opportunity could there be to top up the tanks. These card kits are really easy to make and are a great starting point for anyone who has never made a kit before.*

Kestrel Designs makes a simple kit in N gauge for a typical water tower with a cast-iron tank supported by a brick tower. The pre-coloured plastic parts on three sprues do not necessarily need painting as they are moulded in suitable colours; however, a coat of paint will always improve a plastic model by removing the shiny plastic finish. One kit is shown here, but two kits can be combined to make a much bigger water tower.

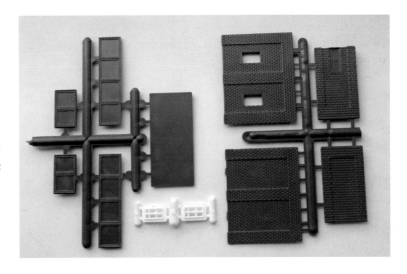

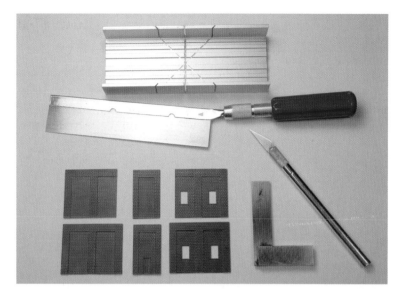

The first step is to remove one corner from each of the longer wall pieces (compare the three pieces upper with those below). The best tool for this to ensure accurate cuts is a razor saw in a mitre block. Alternatively, use a sharp craft knife and an engineer's square; make lots of passes with the knife using light pressure, rather than being heavy handed and trying to cut through the plastic in one go.

RIGHT: The three pieces for the sides can be glued together and joined to end pieces to complete the tower. A piece of plastic card has been cut to size and glued into the top of the tower to form a base for the tank. The tank itself has also been constructed; the sides use two unaltered side pieces and half an end piece (the joints on the inside are filled using thin plastic strip which is then sanded flush). A new bottom for the tank has been made from thin plastic sheet. A piece of thick clear plastic has been cut to size ready to represent the water.

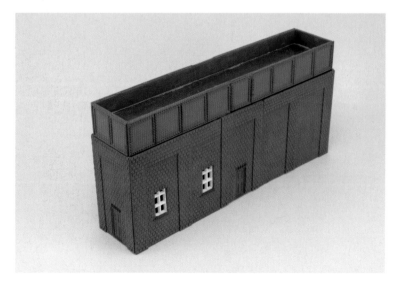

A coat of 'brick-coloured' paint vastly improves the look of the completed model, as does a light dusting with some weathering powders to relieve to the overall colour. The inside of the tank has been painted 'rust colour'. A piece of thick card painted black has raised the 'water level' of the clear plastic to the desired height. Using black paint and clear plastic creates the impression of depth with the water effect.

Other water tanks were open to the elements (you might as well let the rain help to fill the tank). The water level inside the tank can be built up to, say, the halfway mark with a piece of card painted dark brown or black. On this can be placed a piece of clear plastic; any plastic of any thickness will do and packaging material often provides a ready supply of clear material (though be careful to check for scratches). Thicker materials are better, such as a piece of Perspex as this provides a greater illusion of depth, but, whatever you use, the clear plastic will reflect light as if it is water.

The water tank can be simply supported on pillars. These can be made from a core of card or foamboard and clad with brick or stone (either paper or plastic card). Foamboard is a sheet of expanded polystyrene with a thin card backing on both sides. It usually comes in 5mm-thick sheets and it is easy to cut with a sharp knife.

Some water towers were supported on top of a building which may have contained pumping equipment that was used to top up the tank. Such buildings were fairly box-like structures, usually with quite large windows. They are basically an enlarged version of the platelayers' hut and so the same constructional techniques will apply.

PUMPING STATION

Somewhat rarer than a water tower would be a pumping station. Most water towers that needed some help to get the water up into the tank would have contained the necessary pumping equipment in a building that supported the tank. Pumping stations were generally needed when water was a nuisance to the railway.

Such a nuisance would be where water was found where it was not wanted. Usually this was in tunnels,

Water towers are an easy introductory scratch-building project, since the tank is just a box. This OO gauge example has been made from plastic card, but normal card would do just as well. Plastic strip has been used for simple detail and the absence of rivets is not immediately obvious. The supporting pillars are foamboard cores clad in brick-effect plastic sheet. A drinking straw forms the outlet pipe in the middle, while a piece of wire has been used for the filler pipe on the right.

Pumping stations were sometimes found near tunnels in order to remove excess levels of water that could seep through the tunnel bore and would otherwise flood the tunnel and undermine the track. This scene on N-gauge layout 'Barford' uses the very highly detailed Ratio Plastic Models kit for a pumping station, sited right where it is needed, next to the double-track entrance to a tunnel.

where water from above might seep through the tunnel lining and, if not dealt with, would flood the tracks. A compact model of a small pumping station at the lineside, near a tunnel, would make an unusual and interesting feature.

Ratio Plastic Models produces a lovely little kit for a stone-built pumping station, complete with brick chimney in both OO gauge and N gauge. Scratch-building a simple brick building would be only slightly more challenging than building a platelayers' hut, although the typical Victorian arched windows

with many small panes could be a challenge (such windows can be bought in etched brass or plastic).

If you are a GWR modeller, you could include a larger building to represent the ones used in Brunel's failed experiment with atmospheric propulsion. These pumped air out, not water, with the idea that the vacuum so created in a cast tube running under the track would be enough to haul a train. Although quickly abandoned as a working scheme, these buildings stood beside the lineside for many years afterwards.

RIGHT: If you cannot find the exact building you want, cast your search further for another building that can be used instead. For example, a boiler house can easily be used to represent a pumping station. This is the Metcalfe Models OO gauge sand drier building intended for a steam era motive-power depot. All these types of building have a generic appearance, so they can easily be used to represent a pumping station.

BELOW RIGHT: Although the water troughs used in the steam era actually sit between the rails, the associated signs are part of the lineside, as seen at the top left. The signs indicate to the locomotive crew where the start and end of the trough are, so that the water scoop can be lowered and retrieved safely. The troughs and signs are produced as a plastic kit by Ratio Plastic Models in both OO gauge and N gauge.

WATER TROUGHS

A water trough might not be thought of as a lineside detail, since the trough itself goes in the middle of the rails. At the very least, though, it needs a water supply, often a water tower of some description and that would be found at the lineside. There would also be a warning board before the water trough to indicate to the fireman when to lower the scoop. It does make an interesting and rarely modelled feature.

Steam trains are limited to how far they can travel by their need for water, so the invention of the water trough was one of the first steps towards greater long-distance non-stop travel by rail. Taking on water required skill and timing to lower the scoop on the tender into the trough at the right time and to make sure it was raised before the end of the trough. No one has as yet managed to model the flumes of water that were usually seen as an engine took on water. Not all passing locomotives needed water, so one must assume that not every train on the model railway needs a top-up.

Modelling a water trough in either OO gauge or N gauge is quite easy thanks to Ratio Plastic Models, which produces a kit in each scale. Quite a long, straight run is required for even a short water trough, though several kits can be joined together for a more impressive structure. The kit also includes the warning board and this in combination with a model of a water tower would make a striking and unusual feature on a model railway.

TRAVELLING POST OFFICE (TPO) EXCHANGE APPARATUS

One of the challenges that railways face is the stopping and starting of trains to facilitate the transfer of passengers or goods. The time taken to slow down, stop and then get back up to speed can seriously impact on schedules. This was a much greater concern in the steam era, when locomotives did not have the acceleration and braking capabilities of modern rolling stock. How much easier it would be to be able to transfer the cargo without having to stop at all.

The carriage of mail by rail goes back to the very dawn of the railways and it has only recently been lost. Tight schedules are a hallmark of mail trains and the picking up and dropping off of letters while on the move was always a viable option. Indeed, even I.K. Brunel witnessed exchange apparatus in action in 1853. At its height, there were over a thousand daily exchanges taking place until the last one at Penrith on 4 October 1971 signalled the end of an era.

TPO exchange apparatus was often sited away from stations or indeed any obvious signs of habitation, though sometimes within sight of a signal box. This makes them an ideal scene for a lineside model railway that appears to be in the middle of nowhere. Not surprisingly, the site would be somewhere with a considerable length of straight track requiring no obstruction for 229m (250yd) prior to the exchange or 274m (300yd) after it. Only in N gauge could you realistically model these sorts of distances, so a little bit of selective compression is necessary.

The lineside apparatus consisted of two parts, one to receive mailbags and another to despatch them. The collection apparatus was a solid wooden frame with a sturdy net to catch the mailbags. The postal staff on the ground would only extend the net when the mail train was actually due; therefore, it should really be modelled in its collapsed state relative to the variety of other trains that will pass by. The pick-up apparatus was a metal stand that looked a bit like a water crane, though with a shorter arm. These arms were swung out to the track only when the train was due. Access to these tall posts to attach the mailbags was via a ladder, or in some cases a wooden platform. There were often several posts side by side and some posts could hold two mailbags.

Warning boards were placed several hundred yards prior to the exchange apparatus to alert the staff in the TPO coach to be ready. These were either a large board with a yellow zigzag on a white background, or a long board painted white that was laid beside the track.

The final part of the scene was a small hut for the staff of the Post Office (the exchange apparatus was operated by Post Office staff, not railway staff). It would contain a small stove to keep the Post Office employee warm on cold winter nights, as well as a place to stow the actual mailbags; as these were specifically for the transfer to and from speeding trains, they would go no further than the exchange site. Finally, most huts contained a gong that was connected to the nearest signal box, so that the signalman could warn the Post Office employee when the mail train was due.

Bachmann Scenecraft has produced a nice TPO exchange-apparatus set in OO gauge, consisting of pick-up and collection apparatus and a warning board. This model is ready to plant and would be suitable for all railway companies at any time. Despite small improvements in the design and continual attempts to make it more efficient, the basic TPO exchange apparatus never changed appreciably throughout its life, which is good news for the railway modeller.

For those wishing to scratch-build the scene in any scale, there are easy parts and hard ones. The warning boards are easy to make and paint, while the Post Office hut just requires a small hut, usually wooden. Many of the models for platelayers' huts would be suitable, while a straightforward hut is a simple scratch-building project.

The hard part would be the pick-up and collection apparatus. The pick-up posts are not too challenging, as they are basically just a post with a 90-degree bend in the top. This can be made from wire, or brass or plastic tube. The access ladder can be furnished from brass or the plastic ladder that is sold for making signals.

The collection apparatus consists of several sturdy posts. These can be made from real wood or plastic

Bachmann Scenecraft produces a TPO exchange-apparatus set in OO gauge that contains all the necessary elements: equipment for picking up mailbags and setting them down; and a hut for the operator. Scratch-building the apparatus would be a medium skill-level task for most modellers.

Any kind of generic hut (such as a platelayers' hut) would provide the accommodation for the Post Office staff at a TPO exchange site. This is the Dapol OO gauge kit for a coal merchant's office. The only alteration is to remove the merchant's sign from the apex of the roof and replace it with some plastic beading.

strip. The net is more of a challenge, as it is usually very difficult to scale down rope for modelling. However, the net for the collection apparatus was made from very sturdy rope (to withstand the considerable impact) with quite broad holes in the net. It is therefore feasible to use cotton or a very fine string to weave your own net.

DISUSED PLATFORMS

While stations are not strictly considered to be lineside since they are a destination for the railway, a closed station is not a destination by virtue of the fact that it is closed. Railway enthusiasts are all too familiar with the fallout from the Beeching Report;

many stations were closed, even entire routes. Closures on the railway were not a new phenomenon, only the huge scale with which they were carried out under Beeching. The 'Big Four' railway companies and even their constituents prior to 1923 had had no qualms about closing a station if it was not profitable.

Closing a station was meant to save money, yet its complete demolition cost the railway company yet more money. While most stations were obliterated, there were cases where the station was simply closed to the public and left to rot. The station building might be taken down, but very often the platforms were left in situ; they were a reminder to those travelling past that the trains once used to stop at that point.

A disused platform would make a fascinating aspect of a model railway and, of course, the trains do not stop there if you just want to watch them going round and round the layout. If you can build a platform for a working station, there is little difference in building a disused platform.

Kits for platforms are readily available in OO gauge and N gauge, notably those from Peco and Metcalfe Models. The platform faces (the walls that abut the track) need to be made as per the instructions, but the surface requires a little bit more attention. The intention is to portray the impression of abandonment and decay. Weeds, grass and bushes will soon take hold, so the platform needs to look overgrown; you could even plant a small tree in the middle.

The railway still needed to define its boundary, so there might be a mix of existing yet dilapidated fencing, along with newer fencing to keep people and animals out. A few notices to warn people to stay on the right side of the fence could also be added.

ELECTRICAL SUBSTATIONS

The spread of electrification of the railways continues to grow over time, either with overhead lines or a third rail at the side of the track. Some railway lines were electrified at the start of the twentieth century, but it was really the modernization plan of the 1950s that saw the start of the electrification revolution.

Not surprisingly, electrified trains need electricity and just like the power supply to your home, it is stepped down from a higher voltage. To do this, a substation is required.

Electrical substations for the railway are usually placed right beside the railways that they serve. They are an interesting structure to be modelled, as some of the transformers are often out in the open. Bachmann Scenecraft makes an OO gauge substation that has all three of the key elements: a brick building; transformers and electrical equipment in the open; security fencing to keep the public out (and thus safe). The rectangular footprint of this modest all-in-one model would be ideal for locating at the lineside.

It is not too difficult to make your own electrical substation. The brick building is an easy prospect as they are not usually architecturally stimulating; a brick box with a few windows and doors, plus a flat roof, is a simple scratch-building project, ideal for someone who has never tried making a building before.

The electrical equipment is a little more challenging. Transformers with their cooling pipes would be hard to scratch-build. A shortcut is to buy model transformers that are intended as wagon or lorry loads. If you want a bigger transformer than the ones available for your chosen scale, try using the ones for the next scale up, as there is nothing on them to make them look out of scale. Wires and insulators can be made from scraps of wire and plastic.

This neat little model is a ready-to-plant resin casting in the Hornby Lyddle End range for N gauge. A small substation transformer structure like this does not even need to be associated with the power supply for trains, it could be found on non-electrified lines providing power for signals, signal boxes and turnout motors.

This impressive structure from Bachmann Scenecraft is a ready-to-plant building available in OO gauge and N gauge. An electrical substation like this would be most appropriate where there are overhead power lines, or a third rail to provide power to electric trains.

The final element is the security fencing. Older installations would probably have had brick walls around them, which are easy to make from plastic card and brick paper. The more modern sites would be protected by chain-link security fencing, such as the type produced by Ratio Plastic Models and Ten Commandments.

PILLBOXES

Railways are a vital part of any country's war machine, as they transport troops and materials from one place to another. During World War II, when the invasion of the British Isles was a very real threat, defences were prepared at strategic locations to protect this vital infrastructure. Usually, this took the form of a pillbox.

A pillbox is a small structure made from concrete or brick that allows protection for soldiers inside and a means of returning fire via various slits in the structure. They were built beside the railway to protect it from enemy troops. While most of these pillboxes have been demolished, their very solidity has often discouraged their demolition, such that some can still be seen to this day guarding the railway from the lineside. They do not really decay or crumble, just look stained and weather-beaten, possibly overgrown with vegetation.

Ancorton Models makes a kit for a brick pillbox in N gauge, but this would be a very easy structure to scratch-build. They were generally hexagonal with a flat roof, with one door at the rear and thin slits at the front for rifles. The Hornby Skaledale range features

a ready-to-plant pillbox cast in resin. Metcalfe Models makes a twin card kit for a Type 22 and Type 26 Pillbox (square and hexagonal), while Wills makes a plastic kit for a pillbox very similar to the Hornby model.

Given that this is such a basic shape, it is easy to make six walls and a roof from card or plastic sheet. A heavily weathered and overgrown pillbox would make an extremely interesting lineside feature.

Concrete pillboxes were dotted all over the country in World War II to protect vital transport infrastructure in the event of an invasion. They were substantially built and some even remain to this day. An example like this one in the Hornby OO gauge Skaledale range would make an interesting lineside feature half hidden in some undergrowth.

CHAPTER FIVE

TRACK-RELATED FEATURES

Railways need track on which to run, so as this is the very essence of a railway, it is not surprising that a lot of effort goes into maintaining it. In the steam era, this was done largely by manpower alone, with little recourse to machinery. By contrast, the modern era uses some mind-bogglingly complex mobile machinery to do the work, but trackworkers are still required on the ground for checking and certain specialist jobs.

The sartorial appearance of the trackworkers between the two eras forms quite a contrast such that if modelling a very general scene, the apparel of the figures would be enough to inform the viewer of the era without having to see any trains. Modernization has also seen an increasing use of road vehicles to get trackworkers to the track on which they need to work. Finally, all this work often results in waste materials, usually old rails and sleepers. This may be casually discarded by the lineside when the work is complete, waiting to be collected at some point in the future.

STEAM ERA TRACKWORKERS

Maintaining the railway in the steam era was a very labour-intensive process indeed, but as labour was still cheap, this was never a problem. The result is that you would expect to see a lot of people around. Simple maintenance such as lifting and packing, and checking fishplates and keys would have been carried out by a local track gang of about half a dozen men. Major repairs and renewals would have required a lot more men. They used to say that the lightest thing on the railways was the pay packet; a standard 60ft (18m) length of rail would have required twelve men to lift it.

One of the problems with modelling a track gang is that, by necessity, they have to be working on the track. In real life, of course, these men stand safely to one side when a train passes, but this is not possible on a model if you want a working layout and not an unmoving diorama. Therefore, trackworkers are best modelled in non-action poses, standing around by the lineside, as the trains pass them by.

If you want to model the full extent of a track gang in action, you could have them working on a siding or a passing loop instead of the main line. This piece of track need never receive a train; in fact, it could be completely isolated (electrically and physically).

Several manufacturers, such as Langley, Aiden Campbell Miniatures and P&D Marsh, produce suitable figures cast in white metal for OO gauge and N gauge. Peco produces a set of six well-detailed workers for O gauge, including tools. There is the option to affix them to bases to stand them up, but this is not very realistic, so the moulded spigot on one leg is best inserted into a 1.5mm hole in the baseboard.

White metal is a soft lead–tin alloy and the quality of the results can be variable. The softness does mean that some anatomical repositioning of arms and legs is possible, so that figures can be made to suit a specific position and requirement. The figures are best cleaned with a glass-fibre burnishing brush and then sprayed with a metal-specific undercoat; the aerosol cans sold for car body repairs are ideal.

The old Merit track-maintenance party for OO gauge is still available under the Model Scene Accessories brand. These figures come ready-painted, which is helpful if you do not fancy figure painting. They do not stand up so well against more modern ready-painted figures, although they are perfectly acceptable if placed in the distance at the rear of a layout.

Do not restrict yourself just to obviously UK-based manufacturers for figures, as the German companies such as Noch and Preiser produce some exquisite ready-painted figures. Steam era trackworkers were devoid of all the high-visibility clothing of modern times, so a generic model of a man wielding a spade or pickaxe will be right at home. These continental figures are not cheap, but they are worth every penny.

The old Kitmaster sprue of twelve trackworkers is still available courtesy of Dapol. Given that the tooling is about fifty years old, these compare very favourably with the most recent models. This set includes the full range of workers, from the 'gaffer' to men with flags protecting the working party and the workers themselves.

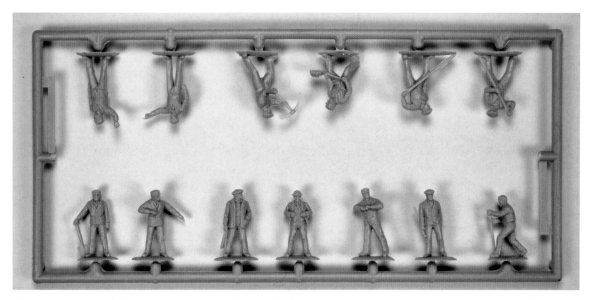

The old Kitmaster OO gauge trackworkers have probably graced thousands of layouts over the last fifty years. They are still available, now produced by Dapol. For their age, they display an extremely high level of detail, which helps to explain their longevity. Counting against them is the fact that they need to be painted and that they stand on rather unsightly bases. Both of these issues are actually quite easy to address.

Once removed from the sprue, the first job is to remove the plastic bases. You can use a craft knife, but a quicker way is to use round-nosed cutters to nibble away the larger parts of the base. Wear eye protection as the small offcuts can ping off in any direction!

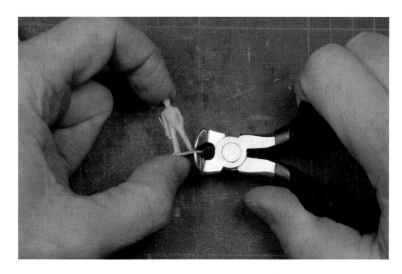

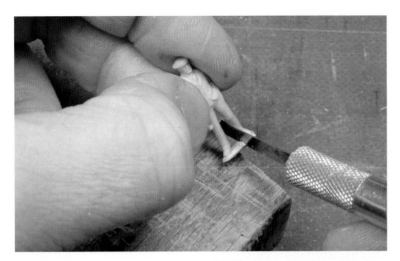

Having nibbled round the plastic base as much as possible, the next step is to make a cut through the base between the legs. A small craft saw or a piece of a razor blade is ideal.

RIGHT: The final pieces of the plastic base can be cut and carved away with a craft knife. Get as close as possible to the feet with the knife, then use a file or some wet & dry sandpaper to finish off.

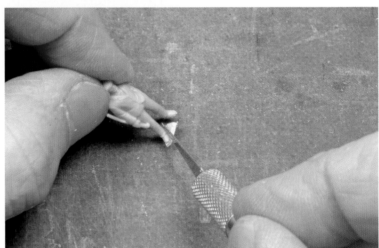

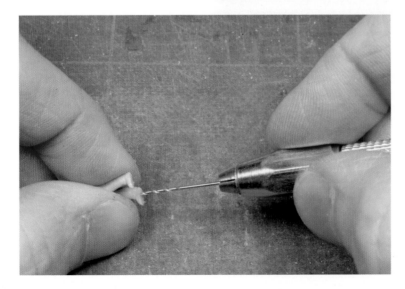

Without their plastic base, the figures will no longer stand up on their own. The figures can be glued to the layout, but a simpler method is to insert a piece of 0.5mm brass wire into one leg. Start by carefully drilling a hole into the plastic. Use a 0.5mm drill bit held in a pin vice, as this gives better control than trying to use an electric mini-drill.

Having drilled a 0.5mm hole into one leg, insert a piece of 0.5mm brass wire. Use pliers to avoid inadvertently bending the wire. A spot of superglue may be necessary to hold the wire in place, but in most cases the wire will be an interference fit that will not require any glue.

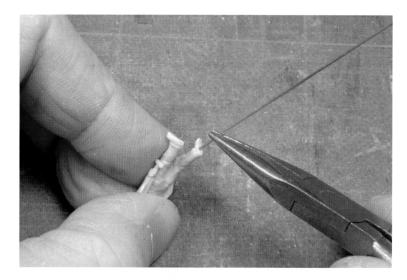

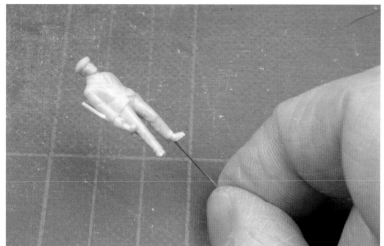

LEFT: Another advantage of adding a piece of brass wire to the figure is that it makes it possible to hold it for painting without having to touch any part of the figure itself. This speeds up the painting process as all areas of the figure can be painted at once, an important consideration when painting a large number of figures.

The brass wire is easy to insert into a piece of foam while the paint dries on the figures, rather than having to lay them flat. This photo shows the starting point for painting, which is an all-over primer of black. This gives a good base on to which to apply the colours for clothing, tools and hair.

Most of the major items of clothing on OO gauge model figures such as this one are fairly easy to paint. The finer details such as face, hands and shirt require a steady hand and a very fine brush, such as an OOO. Skin colour is often difficult to get right and here the paint is white with a touch of red and yellow ochre mixed in.

Here is a selection of the completed OO gauge figures, cruelly enlarged by the camera. Do not worry about getting every last detail painted perfectly; it is not as if you're going to see the whites of their eyes. Once they are installed on the layout as part of an overall scene and observed from normal viewing distance, the slightly impressionistic finish will be more than adequate.

These figures feature a moulded plastic base. This could possibly be blended into the scenery, but a better option is to remove them altogether. This does mean, of course, that the figures will be prone to falling over. A spot of glue will usually hold them upright, but they are very susceptible to accidental knocks. A better alternative is carefully to drill a short hole in one leg and insert a piece of 0.5mm brass wire. This makes it easy to attach the figures to your layout and also to hold them for painting.

Military modellers display great skills when it comes to realistically painting figures. If you want to achieve this level of finish, there are various books on military figure modelling that will show you how. Basic painting is easy to achieve in a few simple steps.

Keep colours muted, as would be appropriate for workers in the steam era, with shades of brown, grey and black, possibly some dark blues for overalls. Skin is always a hard colour to replicate. It is definitely not pink, more a sort of white-cream colour. Experiment with white blended with a touch of red and yellow ochre until you get the right shade. Alternatively, check out the military modelling ranges of paints such as Tamiya and Humbrol for 'flesh' colours. A final step that works well in the large scales of OO gauge and above is to give the figures a wash of well-thinned black paint. This settles into all the nooks and crannies of a well-moulded figure and serves to highlight what would in real life be the shadows of the folds in clothing.

MODERN ERA TRACKWORKERS

Many of the same comments apply to the modern era trackworkers as to the steam era models. The most obvious difference is that modern workers are uniformly dressed in orange high-visibility clothing with hard hats.

Bachmann Scenecraft produces two packs of six workers each in OO gauge and N gauge that are simply exquisite. They come in a variety of poses and the finish is superb, even down to the reflective stripes on the overalls. Some occupy action poses, while others are more statically positioned.

The modern era trackworker is instantly recognizable thanks to hard hats and orange safety wear with reflective stripes. These two packs of ready-painted figures in OO gauge are produced by Bachmann Scenecraft. Incredibly, they are also produced in N gauge and the detail is just as good.

One final comment on figures for the lineside concerns their poses. A figure that is just standing around unmoving will always look realistic, even on a model where only the trains are seen to move. Opinion varies as to the appropriateness of 'action' poses, such as a man forever frozen in time in the middle of wielding a pickaxe over his head.

Such poses emphasize the fact that you are looking at a model, because nothing (apart from the trains) moves, whereas in the real world nothing ever seems to stand still. On the other hand, some modellers believe that even these frozen action poses introduce a certain vibrancy to the scene that the 'standing around doing nothing' figures do not. At the end of the day, it is a matter of personal choice which type of poses you decide to include on your layout.

MAINTENANCE ROAD VEHICLES

The steam era track gangs were local to the section of track that they maintained and their base was a platelayers' hut. This method of working began to decline during the 1960s as the modernization plan started to take hold. As trackworkers became more mobile, they needed a means of getting to the job. Thus began the expansion of the 'man and a van'.

The use of road vehicles in conjunction with track maintenance really started to take off in the 1970s, synonymous with the introduction of the British Rail crew bus in its bright yellow livery. Representative vehicles are available in OO gauge from Oxford Diecast and Base Toys.

The 1980s saw another iconic version of the British Rail crew bus and this was the Ford Iveco truck chassis with bodywork that was both a mess van and a tools and materials store. Kits for this vehicle are available in N gauge from P&D Marsh and Dornaplas.

With the privatization of British Rail, there is less of a unified feel to the vehicles to be seen, as private contractors have often been brought in. Gone are the big yellow trucks, replaced by the 'white van' with either the contractor's logo or Network Rail's own logo. The Ford Transit is the archetypal example of the breed and a superb ready-to-plant model is available from Oxford Diecast.

The bright yellow crew bus for permanent-way workers is an ever-present feature of the lineside from the 1970s onwards. These two OO gauge examples are from Oxford Diecast (left) and Base Toys (right). Remember to provide road access to the lineside for such vehicles, unless they are one of the road–rail types capable of actually travelling on the track.

Vehicles at the lineside are not always large trucks. Small-scale tasks such as one man attending to a signal box may only require a van. Here are three classic van designs produced by Corgi in OO gauge: the Bedford van; the Morris Minor van; and the Ford Transit van.

Even today, permanent-way workers are still getting to the lineside by van and they are still using the Ford Transit van. Gone are the days of all-over yellow, replaced by the omnipresent 'white van' livery, only slightly relieved by the Network Rail logos.

While the modelling of road vehicles may seem to be a peripheral interest in the whole picture of railway modelling, the crew bus or van parked at the side of the track has been very much a part of the modern railway scene and they are often to be glimpsed from a railway carriage. One final thing to remember is some means of access for the road vehicles to get to the track side. Allow for a gate in the boundary fence and even just a rough dirt road down to the lineside.

DISCARDED SLEEPERS AND RAILS

Track maintenance, and in particular track renewal, inevitably produces used materials that have been replaced. As track consists of sleepers, ballast and rails, these are the items that are replaced. With track renewal often carried out against the clock with a 'possession' of the line, the primary aim is to get the track replaced and safe so that trains can start running again. Cleaning up the mess afterwards is not a priority and, if the work overruns, the old parts may be left lying around for another day.

A pile of spent ballast is easy enough to produce, although this was less likely to be seen due to its bulky nature. All that is needed is a pile of model ballast, held in place as ballast on a track would be by using a mix of PVA and water with a drop of washing-up liquid to kill the surface tension.

Remember that there is such a thing as clean ballast and dirty ballast. Fresh ballast tends to look very clean, almost white, while the old ballast is a much darker and dirtier grey. The track should be modelled with the lighter-coloured clean ballast, while a couple of drops of black powder paint in the glue mix for the spent ballast will soon make it look old and dirty.

Lengths of rail are very easy to model, as you can just remove the rails from a few lengths of model track, paint them rust colour, then position them by the lineside. Steam era track used 60ft (18m) lengths of rail and the model rail needs to be cut into scale lengths accordingly.

The modern era has seen the widespread adoption of continuous welded rail, so much longer lengths are appropriate. Despite being made of steel, these long lengths of rail are surprisingly flimsy once they are not held straight and true by the sleepers and chairs. It is common to see the rail lying in quite wavy lines where it has been unceremoniously dumped by the lineside.

Having removed the rail from some model track to lay by the lineside, you might think that the model sleepers that are left over can be used to represent a pile of old sleepers. This does not always work so well, because model track is made to be either solidly sectional or flexibly bendy. The model sleepers are joined by a webbing to keep them the correct distance apart; this is easily removed, but sometimes the sleepers have holes under the chairs to aid the flexibility. Plastic sleepers can often be far too thick (they are made this way for strength and durability). This is not a problem when they are properly ballasted, but they do not look right on their own.

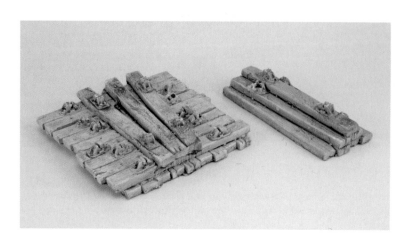

Piles of sleepers are often to be found by the lineside either before or after maintenance and renewal work. These well-detailed sleepers are cast in plaster by Ten Commandments and only require painting to finish. They represent the 'after' pile of sleepers as the chairs are still attached. The ones shown here are for O gauge.

Some modellers prefer to hand-build their track from individual components. In this case, the sleepers are usually much more to scale and may even be available without the chairs moulded on. The chairs that are used to hold the rail on real track may be available as separate castings, though in model form they tend to be just cosmetic. The final option for sleepers without chairs is to use the correct size of rectangular plastic strips, such as sold by Plastruct and Evergreen Scale Models.

As you probably just want a couple of small piles of used sleepers, perhaps the easiest approach of all is to use the well-detailed castings available from Ten Commandments in OO gauge and O gauge. These plaster castings need painting, but this offers the opportunity to apply a really well-weathered finish to the sleepers and some rust-coloured paint to the chairs.

CABLE DRUMS

Given the amount of cabling that is required to be installed along the railway track, it is not surprising that you might see a few cable drums lying around. In the steam era, the thousands of telegraph poles would have needed to be connected with wire. In the modern era, cabling for signals and turnouts is routed through concrete trunking, while electric traction requires overhead wires supported by masts and gantries.

You can make a passable cable drum by quite simply cutting out two circles of card and gluing them to a small piece of rod; wooden dowelling is ideal, or a section

from an old ballpoint pen. Discarded cable drums by the lineside would likely be empty, though you can add the cable if required. The thin wire used by modellers to wire up their layouts can be wrapped round the core of the cable drum. The drawback to using plain card is that there is no representation of the planking or bolts from which real cable drums are made, although you could use planked plastic card instead.

The Model Scene Accessories track gang includes a very nice plastic cable drum, of the type that is covered around the circumference to protect the cable inside. These cable drums are available in N gauge and OO gauge. They are made from red plastic that can be weathered to tone it down and they also have some 'cable' wrapped inside.

York Modelmaking produces simple kits for cable drums in O gauge, OO gauge and N gauge. These are laser-cut from real wood. This has the advantage that the cable drums do not need to be painted, yet they look like real wood. Freshly made and distributed cable drums would look like clean wood; older ones would be dirtier and this can be achieved with a light wash of thinned black paint that will stain the wood and age it.

BALLAST BINS

Another steam era feature was the ballast bins that were to be found at intervals along the lineside. When track maintenance was the preserve of local track gangs operating from a platelayers' hut, they needed a local source of materials. Sometimes, a bit

The laser-cutting specialist York Modelmaking manufactures cable-drum kits in all the major scales. As the drums are made from wood, they look realistic without any further work, although you can weather them if you wish. The ones shown here are for N gauge and they display a high level of detail, despite the larger of the two sizes being smaller than a 1p coin.

of fresh ballast was needed when lifting and packing the track to maintain a smooth ride, so, rather than having to call up a wagonload of ballast, it was more convenient to have it immediately and locally available.

While some ballast bins were made from brick, the majority were made from wood, often using old sleepers. They were extremely simple affairs and would be very easy to scratch-build using lengths of rectangular-section plastic strip. If you still want a ready-to-plant version, Ten Commandments makes some nice models in OO gauge and O gauge.

In later years, preformed concrete sections were used to make ballast bins to a standard design. One of these would perhaps form the easiest scratch-building project of all, since it consists merely of a floor, a back wall, two sloping side walls and a low front wall. You could use whatever material you are most comfortable with, be it plastic sheet or just plain card. The latter often can be sourced from old writing pads, which would have the advantage of having a little texture to represent the concrete, as well as being a grey 'concrete' colour. With a little weathering and the addition of some ballast, this is a project that really could be completed within an hour.

Ballast bins came in all shapes and sizes, but often resembled the coal staithes found in goods yards for coal merchants. Therefore, there is no reason why a model of a coal staith cannot be used as a ballast bin, as here in N gauge using a resin casting produced by Ten Commandments. Note how the fresh ballast is cleaner and therefore a different colour to the well-used ballast that's actually on the track.

This plaster-cast ballast bin is made by Ten Commandments for O gauge. It is typical of the simple yet robust design made from old sleepers often found in the steam era. This model just requires painting to finish. Ballast is moulded inside, but this could be topped up with the actual ballast used on your layout.

CHAPTER SIX

SIGNALLING

The signalling infrastructure of railways is very much a lineside feature and an evocative symbol of trains, even to the non-enthusiast. However, it is more than just a symbol, since it is an essential part of safely controlling a railway and the people who use it. Besides the signals themselves, there are the signal boxes that control them, the control wires for signals and rodding for turnouts and, in more modern times, the relay cabinets and concrete trunking associated with colour light signals.

It is hard to imagine a railway without signals, but signals were not invented when the railways were born. It is sobering to think of the earliest railways running without signals. They simply used the time-interval system, whereby it was assumed to be safe to despatch another train to follow the first one after a certain amount of elapsed time. Not surprisingly, there were numerous accidents and lives lost. The rapid spread of railway development as part of the Victorian mania for railways necessitated a better system than just a policeman waving a flag. Thus was born the signalling system that remains largely unchanged to this day, despite the modernization from semaphore signals to colour lights, and even the abolition of localized signal boxes.

WHERE TO PLACE SIGNALS

The Victorian railway engineers developed the concept of rigidly and safely controlling the railway. Central to this concept within the limits of Victorian technology was the idea of breaking the railway lines up into clearly defined sections (also known as 'blocks' or 'block sections') under the control of one person (the signalman). Each block section communicated with the next, effectively passing trains between them. Only the signals within a block can be controlled by its signalman.

The length of block sections really depended on where they were and the frequency of trains. Busy urban areas with frequent trains had short blocks, while sleepy branch lines with just a couple of trains per day would have long blocks. Railway modellers tend to think of signals as being something you only see at stations. Many stations have signals, but there could be many block sections between stations, thus necessitating signals and signal boxes for each one. As the transition from one block to another could be in the middle of nowhere, it is perfectly justifiable to have a signal box and signals miles from anywhere; in other words on any section of lineside modelled without a station.

Another place to find signals would be at a junction where the railway line diverges to two different destinations. Junctions did not always have stations and they could be in the middle of nowhere. Even a passing loop would have needed to be signalled, thus requiring signals and a signal box.

The placement of signals at a station is beyond the scope of this book, but it is worth looking at some simple signalling at places that could be found between the stations. The simplest situation would be the basic block section on a railway line. A signalman cannot pass a train forward to the next block until the signalman in that block informs him that his line is clear such that he can accept the train. If the next block is not clear, the signalman in the first block needs to hold his train and for this he would simply have a stop signal (possibly with a distant signal to forewarn the train driver).

In terms of modelling the lineside, this is easily represented by having a signal box and a stop signal. If you have a long enough track to model, you may be able to include the distant signal, or you could just include the distant signal without the need for a signal box.

At a junction, it is necessary to indicate to the train driver which route he will take (although the driver really ought to know where is he is going; the signal actually informs him that it is safe to proceed). Not surprisingly, therefore, a junction will have a junction signal, which is really just two signals combined into one, one for each of the two possible routes. The opposite direction will also be protected by signals to avoid conflicting movements where tracks cross over each other.

The semaphore signal is instantly recognizable as a piece of railway infrastructure, even to those who are not interested in trains. This fine example controls the entrance to Ramsbottom Station from Rawtenstall on the East Lancashire Railway. At first glance, this may look like a junction signal as one post is taller than the other, but it actually controls which of the two platforms to use, as bidirectional running is possible for both platforms. Note the two smaller arms lower down, which are shunt signals.

A passing loop is similar to a junction, in that there are two possible routes for the train to take. In this case, the train driver does not necessarily know which route he will take, since trains are not always recessed into a passing loop; it depends on whether there is a faster train behind that needs to overtake it.

Many modellers see signalling as one of the black arts of model railways that are too bewildering to get to grips with. This leads some modellers to omit signals altogether, or merely to include a token few, possibly incorrectly positioned. An open stretch of railway does not need signals like a station does (unless there is a junction or passing loop), so often it is just a case of including a signal or two if you want them to define a block section.

SEMAPHORE SIGNALS

The traditional semaphore signal is a piece of railway infrastructure that will be familiar to virtually all railway enthusiasts. The moving arm of the signal is red with a white stripe for a stop signal, and yellow with a black chevron and notched end for a distant signal. The horizontal position is uniformly used to indicate 'stop' (also known 'danger' or 'on'). The angled position is known as the 'off' position (or 'clear') and indicates that it is clear to proceed.

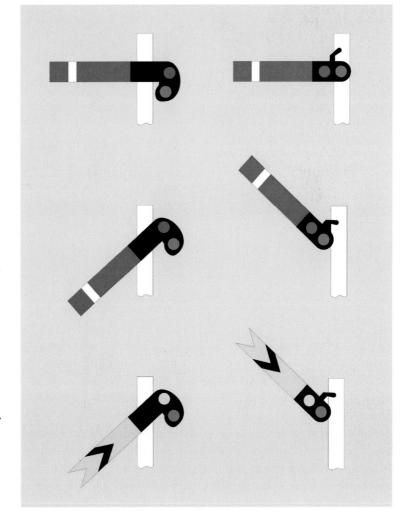

The two types of semaphore signal are shown: lower quadrant on the left and upper quadrant on the right. The bottom two signals are distant signals (the others are home signals). The top two signals show 'danger' (the others show 'clear'). Note the different design for the coloured lenses between upper and lower quadrant types, so that the correct colour aligns with a lamp behind to display the correct aspect as the signal moves. If the signal wire breaks, an upper quadrant signal naturally falls to 'danger', while a lower quadrant signal is pivoted and weighted so as to pull the arm up to the 'danger' position.

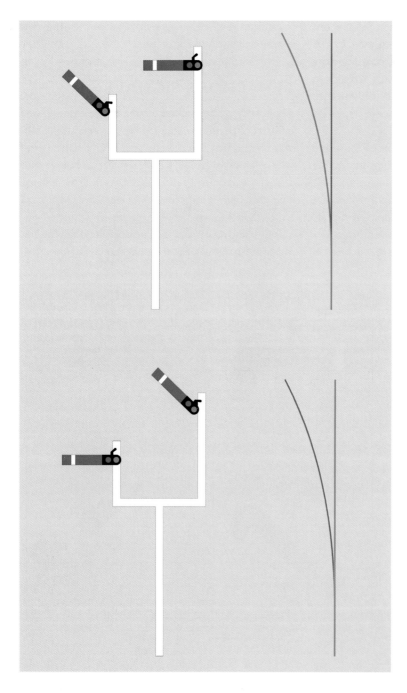

A simple junction consists of a main line and a diverging line (the latter usually being the one that curves away from the straight line). A bracketed junction signal is used to control trains approaching such a junction. The shorter arm denotes the diverging route, while the taller arm is used for the main line. Both signals can display 'danger' but only one at a time can display 'clear' and that will be dependent upon the route selected. Real signal boxes use mechanical interlocking to prevent showing the incorrect signal for the route that is set.

This 45-degree angle can be up or down (respectively known as upper quadrant or lower quadrant). The difference is not indicative of anything other than the railway company whose signal it is, since each one tended to favour entirely upper or lower quadrant; most favoured the former, but some, notably the Great Western Railway and the North Eastern Railway, chose the latter.

The posts that held the signal arm were much more varied and, once again, broadly indicative of the railway company that installed them. The paint scheme was always white, with just the bottom of the post painted black. Wooden posts were used at first, but some railway companies used tubular steel, lattice posts or even old pieces of rail. The posts were often topped off with a decorative finial.

Semaphore signals can be fiddly things to build, especially in the smaller scales; getting them to work can be even harder. The trouble with semaphore signals is that, by their very nature, the signals give a visual representation of the instruction to the train driver. If the signals are not working, it means having trains make illegal moves at signals, either stopping at a clear signal, or passing a signal at danger (the infamous SPAD, or Signal Passed At Danger).

There is actually no shortage of signal kits for most of the major scales from Ratio Plastic Models, Langley Models, P&D Marsh and Model Signal

Hornby has produced some simple ready-made signals in OO gauge for many years. This single-post distant signal has an upper quadrant arm attached to a slotted post (a post consisting of two halves with crosspieces to join them). On real railways, there is quite a distance between signals, far greater than there would be room for on an average model railway. A distant signal might be found by the lineside without the need to model a signal box close by.

This Hornby OO gauge junction signal is of the lattice-post type (from the lattice of cross-webbing that joins two outer strips). This signal shows that the diverging route is to the left (and, correctly, only one arm can ever be 'off', although both can be at 'danger'). The shorter post and the platform can be removed from this model and reinstalled on the right-hand side of the post if your model has a diverging route on the right.

Engineering. The material used in these kits varies from plastic to brass to white metal. Some can easily be made to work, while with others it is more difficult. Encouragingly, the various types of signal post, such as wooden, tubular and lattice, are all available, so if you stringently model a particular time and place, appropriate signals will be available to suit.

Many signals were fairly standard in terms of size, especially those in open areas that defined the start of a block section. Others, though, were quite different and were made to a specific arrangement to suit a particular location. An example would be an extra-tall signal post, so that the signal could be seen clearly over a visual obstruction such as a bridge. Most signal kits can be altered to some extent, but if you really want to go in for bespoke working signals, you should seek out the massive range of parts available from Model Signal Engineering.

The recently introduced range of working signals from Dapol in OO gauge and N gauge were a welcome boost for many modellers. The range covers by far the most common signals, namely the Great Western Railway lower quadrant and the London Midland and Scottish Railway upper quadrant, with both stop and distant signals available for both. These motorized signals are simple to install, including the wiring, and they even incorporate an LED to illuminate the spectacle plate as the arm moves.

COLOUR LIGHT SIGNALS

While semaphore signalling has been around for well over a hundred years and there are examples still to be seen on the real railways today, most semaphore signals have given way to colour light signals as part of modernization and renewal work. Colour light signals are not a recent innovation, though, with the first examples being seen on the Liverpool Overhead Railway as far back as 1920.

There is quite a variety of colour light signals in terms of the actual number of colour lights they use (referred to as the number of 'aspects'). The simplest have just two lights (red for stop below green for proceed) and are thus known as 'two-aspect' signals. The addition of a yellow light for 'caution' gives a 'three-aspect' signal. A second yellow light above the green light is a 'four-aspect' signal; that second yellow serves to warn of the next signal's primary yellow indication.

Unlike semaphore signals, with colour light signals there is no concept of stop and distant signals. With two- and three- aspect signals, the stop and distant signals are rolled into one, as each signal is capable of indicating the status of the next signal.

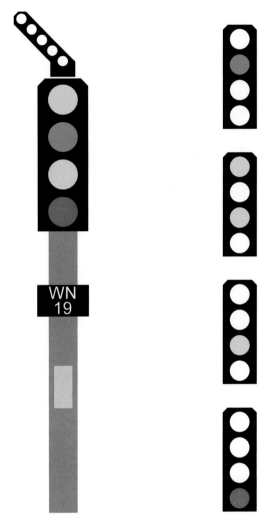

This diagram shows on the left a typical four-aspect colour light signal controlling the approach to a junction. The five angled white lights on the top are the 'feather' that illuminates when the diverging route is selected. The four signal heads on the right show the sequence of illumination of four successive signals (green, double yellow, yellow and red).

Another difference with colour light signals is at junctions, whereby in order to simplify the amount of information on display to drivers, the signal for the diverging route was dispensed with altogether. In its place is a set of five white lights atop the signal arranged at 45 degrees and thus pointing left or right to correspond to the direction in which the route

These ultra-modern signals are at Huyton in Liverpool and, like many things today, multiple LEDs have replaced a single-aspect bulb. This means that just two lenses are now required to display the four possible aspects. The lower lens can show red, green or yellow, while the upper lens shows just yellow for when a 'double yellow' display is required. The left-hand signal has a feather to indicate a diverging route to the left. Note the different design of the two signals, the right-hand one having a ladder and platform. STUART BARDSLEY

diverges. These sets of white lights are commonly known as 'feathers' and they only illuminate when the diverging route is set and when the signal is not at 'danger'.

A final difference with colour light signals is that they are not always situated within sight of a signal box. Their electrical rather than mechanical nature means that they can be much further away from the signal box, the extreme now being several concentrated signalling centres that are often hundreds of miles away from some of the signals that they control. Modernization has made most signal boxes redundant, but although they are no longer used, many signal boxes can still be seen in a disused and boarded-up state by the lineside.

For modellers, colour light signals are a bit easier to install as working models since they have no mechanical parts. If you are comfortable with layout wiring, installing colour light signals will not prove to be difficult. This is helped by a wide range of ready-to-plant signals in both OO gauge and N gauge, covering two-, three- and four-aspect signals, even junction signals with feathers. Among the various manufacturers, some of the most popular products are those by Berko and Eckon.

If the wiring of these signals still concerns you, you can just install non-working dummy signals. Although they do not light up, this manifestation of non-working is actually a lot less obvious than the mechanically visual indication of a semaphore signal.

The widespread use of colour light signals and large power boxes covering hundreds of square miles has led to the demise of most traditional signal boxes. Some survive as listed buildings, some are demolished, while others are left to deteriorate. The latter is represented by this OO gauge resin model that is ready to plant from Bachmann Scenecraft.

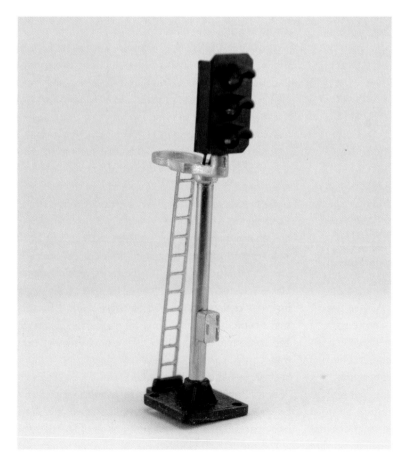

One of the advantages of colour light signals over semaphore signals from a modelling point of view is that they are easier to make operational. The two wires just visible below the signal head that disappear into the post show that this is a working model signal. It is all the more impressive when you consider that this three-aspect example from Berko is actually in N gauge.

This four-aspect signal manufactured by Berko is for OO gauge. It is very easy to install by drilling a small hole into the baseboard for the wires that come out of the base. This is a very good model of a typical prototype, though the silver paint on the post is uncharacteristic; it is a simple job to repaint this in a more appropriate 'battleship grey' colour.

Model Scene Accessories makes a simple generic non-working three-aspect colour light signal in plastic and it even comes with a relay cabinet. There is a feather moulded above the signal lights indicating a line diverging to the right. If your line diverges to the left, you will need to cut the feather off, turn it through 90 degrees and reattach it to the signal. The plain black plastic can be painted appropriate colours, namely, light grey for the post and black for the signal head.

SIGNAL BOXES

It is almost true that no layout is complete without at least one signal box. Even a layout that just models the lineside without any stations or junctions can still justify a small signal box in order to control a block section. Signal boxes came in a seemingly infinite variety, yet their style and architecture could once again be used to define the railway company that built them, just like the signals themselves.

Some very small signal boxes were single storey, usually mounted on a platform at a station, but the greater majority of signal boxes were two-storey affairs (one or two were even taller in order to provide sighting over an obstruction such as a bridge). The classic two-storey arrangement served a dual purpose. Obviously the first one was the good view of the line that the elevated second storey provided. The second was to house the locking equipment in the ground-floor portion of the building (this part of the signal box is often simply referred to as the 'locking room'). The locking equipment was basically all of the mechanics that provide interlocking of the levers (to prevent dangerous or conflicting movements).

Constructional styles of signal boxes varied considerably. Some were all-wood affairs, while some were all-brick and others were a mix of the two, usually a brick ground floor and a wooden upper floor. Roof styles were equally varied, with gabled roofs, hipped roofs and flat roofs. Access to the upper floor was traditionally by means of an external stairway and landing, though some of the more modern signal boxes had the stairs internally. The size of the signal box was basically governed by the number of levers that needed to be accommodated, so busy junctions and stations would be long affairs, while signal boxes that controlled just a couple of signals for a block section would be quite small.

Some railway companies built modular-style signal boxes that could be built as multiples of the same basic parts depending on the number of levers to be accommodated. Even without an obviously modular

RIGHT: *Model Scene Accessories produces a pack of two ready-made colour light signals in OO gauge that only require painting. While they are non-functioning, the lack of actual working lights will be acceptable to some modellers, not least for the simplicity of having no wiring to contend with. The inclusion of a relay cabinet in the pack is a nice touch.*

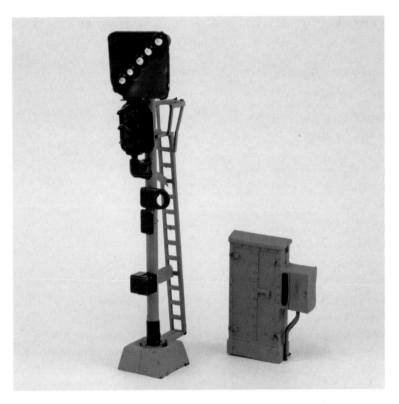

BELOW: *The classic British signal box is a fairly standard shape in terms of a control cabin atop a locking room. Yet within this, there is a huge variety of designs in terms of construction material, roof style, length, windows, verandas and so on. This example is an all-wooden affair at Darley Dale on the Peak Rail preserved railway.*

Some signal boxes were quite ornate affairs, reflecting the extravagance of quality that many railway companies displayed as part of their projection of image. This example is on the preserved Yorkshire Dales Railway. Note the two different warning signs at the end of the platform – one is pre-war, while the other is utterly modern.

OPPOSITE PAGE, TOP: **Many traditional signal boxes are now over a hundred years old and, as such, they are showing their age. Those that are not governed by listed-building regulations have seen some modernization. This is an interesting view of the side and rear of Rainford Junction signal box, which is still in use today. The brickwork of the locking room has been shored up with timber framing. There are other details such as the windows covered by vandal-proof meshing, the vents for gas heaters, a very modern street light and the replacement of all wooden stair and veranda rails with metal square tube section that has been bolted together.**

RIGHT: **This view from the train on the Yorkshire Dales Railway shows a classic junction signal. The shorter post indicates the diverging route into the loop on the left. The longer post with the signal in the 'clear' position shows that the right-hand track is the main line. The signal box would make an interesting model, as it is only used when a more intensive service requires the use of the loop. At all other times, the windows are protected by modern steel roller shutters.**

concept, most railway company signal boxes had an obvious family resemblance no matter how large or small. Remember also that the railway companies did not build all their own signal boxes, as some were provided by the independent signalling equipment manufacturers such as Saxby and Farmer.

All of this architectural variety means that the first task for the railway modeller is to decide whether or not to adopt a specific design or type of signal box in order to portray a certain time and place. If you choose to be broadly freelance in your approach, then you have a huge selection of signal boxes to choose from, many available as ready-to-plant models or kits.

Despite the similarity of signal boxes built by the same railway company, many also resembled the signal boxes of other companies (since they were a building performing the same function), so a kit for one company's signal box may do for another. After the application of the specific company paint scheme, it may be hard to tell the difference. Most railway companies used signalling contractors at some point, so one of the latter's standard signal box styles may be appropriate anywhere in the country.

READY-TO-PLANT SIGNAL BOXES

Companies like Bachmann Scenecraft and Hornby (under the Skaledale and Lyddle End banners in OO gauge and N gauge respectively) have produced a wide range of ready-to-plant signal boxes in recent years. These are usually cast in resin to a high standard and painted as appropriate. Most are based on actual prototypes, so they are very accurate; indeed, some of the prototype signal boxes are fully restored and maintained on preserved railways.

Quite literally, all you have to do with these ready-to-plant models is take them out of their often

This London and South Western Railway signal box by Bachmann Scenecraft in OO gauge is fully finished and ready to plant. The model represents an all-stone construction apart from the windows, while the hipped roof and wooden veranda add unique character. Note the small locking room windows and the gap at foundation level for turnout rodding and signal wires.

This is a very typical signal box design by Bachmann Scenecraft, completed ready-to-plant in British Railways steam era Midland Region colours. The locking room is of brick construction, the signal cabin is wood and the roof is a simple apex with gable ends. On this particular OO gauge model, the roof can be removed so that you can add interior detail, such as the lever frame, table and chairs and a stove and, of course, a signalman.

Bachmann Scenecraft's extensive range of ready-to-plant signal boxes is completed by this modern signal box. The angular walls and flat roof give it a utilitarian yet stylish appearance. A box like this would likely have been built as part of the 1950s modernization plan and as such is likely to control signals and turnouts electrically, thus avoiding the need for mechanical interlocking, turnout rodding and wires.

In rare cases, a signal box has had to be temporarily replaced due to damage or reconstruction work and what better to use as a temporary structure than a Portakabin. This two-level affair in OO gauge from the Bachmann Scenecraft range would still give the signalman a classic elevated view of the line. If you don't fancy a Portakabin as a signal box, you can always justify one as accommodation for permanent-way staff – the modern equivalent of the platelayers' hut.

substantial packaging and put them on to your layout. The level of finish is such that there is often very little to be done to improve them. This is perhaps not much of a challenge for the railway modeller who likes to make things, but there is no denying that ready-made buildings are a huge timesaver.

There is, though, a lack of individuality to layouts that are all using the same models. Having said that, there is no reason why you cannot repaint one of these models to suit a specific time and place, thus individualizing a mass-produced model. The fact that these models are ready-made and hand-finished does mean that they are much more expensive, so it seems a shame to pay for this only to repaint it yourself. A much cheaper alternative might be to make up a signal box kit instead.

KIT-BUILT SIGNAL BOXES
The railway modeller is even better served for signal boxes by turning to kits rather than ready-to-plant

models. These kits are enjoyable to make and obviously you now have access to the interior of the building, which means you can also provide a detailed interior with levers and signalman, perhaps even some lighting to show it off, something that is not possible with many of the ready-made models. All the major modelling scales are served by a good range of kits covering a range of actual railway companies and architectural styles.

Starting with card kits, the Superquick Model Kits signal box in OO gauge has been available for many decades and this average-sized signal box must have graced countless layouts. The external stairs are provided as a plastic moulding, as this flimsy-looking part of the overall model might otherwise be difficult to make from card alone. Having said that, the master of the card kit, Metcalfe Models, produces two kits in OO gauge and N gauge, with card steps that with care can be constructed to produce very convincing models.

Like the Superquick Model Kits signal box, another kit that has been around for about fifty years is the former Kitmaster (later Airfix and now Dapol) all-wooden signal box with hipped roof. This makes up into a modest-sized signal box, though the hipped roof makes it difficult to join two kits together to create a larger structure, unlike the gabled designs with simple sloping roofs. The kit is a little basic by modern standards, but that just means there is room to detail and personalize the model. The wooden ground floor is easily converted to brick by overlaying with brick paper or embossed plastic sheet. An interesting conversion would be to build this kit as a boarded-up disused signal box on a modern era layout.

In N gauge, Kestrel Designs produces a simple generic signal box that would be useful for a lineside situation where it was simply controlling a block section. Also in N gauge, Peco offers an accurate model of a Saxby and Farmer signal box design. This is an extremely well-produced kit and it even includes a detailed interior. These kits can be joined together to produce a longer signal box without too much difficulty. Ancorton Models produces an N gauge kit for a Lancashire and Yorkshire Railway signal box; this is slightly different in that it is produced from laser-cut plywood.

Peco also produces a modern-style brick-built signal box in OO gauge with a flat roof. By contrast, Wills produces a kit for a more traditional steam era all-wooden signal box.

Metcalfe Models produces a number of superb signal box models in N gauge and OO gauge. This N-gauge version of a large signal box is a classic brick and timber design. The level of detail and finish in the smaller scale is most impressive.

The signal box kit currently marketed by Dapol can trace its origins back fifty years through ownership by Airfix and originally Kitmaster. Being in continuous production all this time means that it has appeared on many hundreds of layouts. With some simple alterations, the kit can be built as a disused signal box that looks sufficiently individual on any layout. There are only a few parts, which makes this an ideal 'kit-bashing' project for a beginner.

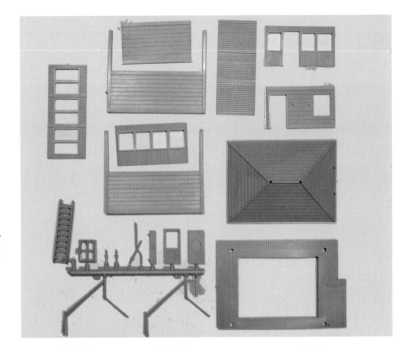

LEFT: *Most signal boxes have windows at the front of the lower storey rather than the side. The position of some new windows is marked on the rear of the front piece, then a side piece is used as a template to mark out the window openings. A fine-tipped marker pen rather than pencil is used for ease of drawing on plastic.*

The plastic in the kit is quite thick for cutting with just a craft knife, so an Olfa cutter (shown on the right) is used with a small engineer's square to keep everything straight. An Olfa cutter effectively gouges rather than cuts, which makes it easier to penetrate thicker plastic. An ordinary craft knife and a file are used to clean up the openings once the plastic has been removed.

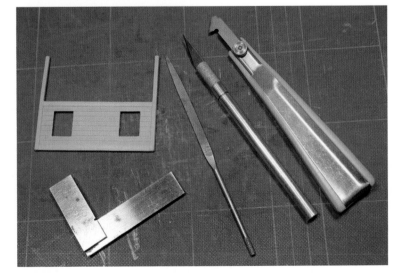

The Dapol kit represents an all-wooden signal box, so in order to introduce some uniqueness to the model the ground floor will be given a brick finish. Once the four sides have been glued together, some thin plastic sheet is used to cover the plank effect. This is thin enough to be able easily to cut out the door and window openings once it has been glued into place. The plastic sheet also makes all four sides flush with the corner posts. Note how the window next to the door has been covered up as a further alteration to the kit.

RIGHT: The brick effect can be achieved using either embossed plastic sheet or one of the many brick paper products that are available. Plastic sheet has moulded mortar lines and is more realistic, though only when the model is viewed closely. It is also harder to disguise the joints at the corners. Brick paper can be easily folded to 90 degrees, which means that one continuous piece of paper can be cut out of a sheet to go seamlessly around all four corners.

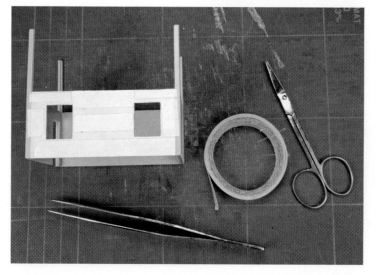

LEFT: There are various methods for attaching brick paper to a plastic model. Glue sticks and PVA are inadvisable as they tend to be difficult to apply evenly, resulting in lumps and bumps. A liquid polystyrene glue, as used to join the plastic parts, can be brushed over the paper once placed on the model and this will effectively melt the back of the paper on to the plastic. If you use this approach, make sure that you do it in a very well-ventilated room due to the amount of fumes produced. A simple method is to use very thin double-sided sticky tape, strips of which are laid on the model, and then the backing is removed with tweezers.

Most ground-floor windows were bricked up during World War II as a precaution against damage from air raids. In many cases, a different brick was used to the one that the signal box was built with. This is easily done on the model by using a brick paper from another manufacturer. The paper is attached to a piece of card with double-sided sticky tape and then glued behind the window openings.

LEFT: With the ground floor completed, the upper storey is added and given a primer coat of Humbrol 'wood colour'. The kit does not include a floor, so one has been added from a piece of card. As the staircase is a potentially fragile item, the model has been glued to a card base that will protect it while the model is completed. The fourth step on the stairs has been deliberately broken as part of the abandoned look. Note the cut-out at the front where the turnout rodding and signal wires would leave the locking room.

Broken glass is quite difficult to achieve in model form as it is difficult to break the clear plastic glazing material in a realistic way. A small hole was cut into each window, which was then gradually enlarged with random cuts and a small pair of scissors until the desired effect was achieved. One set of windows has been boarded up – this is just a piece of thin textured card painted with Humbrol 'wood colour' and then given a dusting of black weathering powder.

There is an air of dereliction about the completed signal box. There are weeds growing by the steps, broken windows, faded paintwork and weathered slates on the roof. The changes to the ground floor and the abandoned look of the upper floor mean that it is hard to recognize that this is the popular Dapol kit. A little bit of individuality is pleasing to achieve and it sets your layout apart from all the rest.

One of the widest ranges of plastic signal box kits comes from Ratio Plastic Models. Its GWR wooden signal box kit is available in both OO gauge and N gauge, an interesting prototype, not least because the stairway is inside the building. A fully detailed interior is provided with the kit and this is available as a separate kit for those who wish to detail the interior of another signal box kit. Ratio Plastic Models produces two other OO gauge kits, one for a brick and wood GWR signal box and one for a Midland Railway signal box.

SCRATCH-BUILDING A SIGNAL BOX
Despite the wide range of suitable signal box models available as kits or ready-to-plant models, there are occasions when it is preferable to scratch-build a signal box. It might be that you are modelling exactly a real place and that the unique signal box is a signature

Wills produces a lovely plastic kit in OO gauge for an all-wooden construction signal box. The sliding front windows can be modelled in the open position if desired, as seen here. No interior detailing is supplied, but kits are available for this from Ratio Plastic Models and Peco. Note the ramp that would cover the signal wires and point rodding so that railway workers could safely walk in front of the signal box.

part of the location. Even if you are freelancing your layout based on the practices of a real railway company, it might be that you need a particular style of signal box, or an exact size of signal box to fit a particular location.

There are plenty of published drawings for signal boxes in order to obtain the correct dimensions. These can be followed exactly, or used as a guide to build a larger or smaller signal box, given the modular appearance of similar signal boxes on the same railway route or region.

The obvious starting point is to build the locking room, the ground-floor portion of the building. Brick was the most popular material for this part and a basic wall shape is easily made with a door at one end and windows at the front and rear. Bear in mind that many signal boxes had these ground-floor windows bricked up during World War II as a precaution against bomb damage. Remember to include a gap in the bottom couple of courses of bricks at the front of the building, as this would be where the point rodding and signal wires would exit the building.

The most popular material for the upper floor was wood; planked plastic sheet or scored card are both suitable. The biggest challenge to the upstairs part of a signal box is the necessarily large windows at the front and sides (one side will usually have a door for access). One option is to glue thin rectangular plastic section to a sheet of clear material. Be careful which glue to use, since inevitably a certain amount may leak out, so a clear-drying glue is less obtrusive. Some polystyrene glues for plastic can cause clear plastic sheet to 'fog'.

An alternative is carefully to cut out a 'lace doily' of all the window bars from a piece of thin card. A final option is to cut thin strips from self-adhesive mailing labels, which are easily stuck to a piece of clear material to represent the glazing. As most window bars were painted white on the real thing, there is no need to paint them on the model, as the labels are already white. Painting such thin strips can otherwise be a fiddly task.

For the roof, slates or tiles were usually the order of the day, with only a few designs (usually post-war) utilizing a flat roof. If you want an ultra-realistic roof you can cut and fit individual slates, which is not as arduous a task as you might imagine on the relatively small roof of a signal box. Less taxing but just as realistic is to use strips of thin card or thick paper with notches cut in them to represent the gaps between slates.

Avoid the cliché of cracked or broken slates, since the railway companies kept their buildings in good order and such damage would have been fixed quickly. Embossed plastic sheet representing slates is available from Slater's Plastikard; this makes roofing quick and simple and the finish can be quite realistic. Last of all, the likes of Superquick Model Kits and Metcalfe Models produce sheets of printed slates and tiles. These lack the relief of all the other methods but they are pre-coloured quite credibly.

All signal boxes featured at least a stove (which requires a flue showing through the roof), while most had a proper fireplace to keep the signalman warm on the long winter nights, for which a brick chimney was provided at the rear of the structure. This is easily made using embossed or paper brick sheets over a former made from thick card.

Perhaps the trickiest part of scratch-building a signal box is the stairway, with its delicate combination of treads and handrails. The stairway can be scratch-built from pieces of plastic strip, which is not too bad since they are not usually very big stairways up to a signal box. Plastruct makes plastic stair treads and separate handrails in OO gauge and N gauge that can be cut to length and easily make up a stairway. The safety rail on the landing is easily created from plastic strip. Finally, you could use parts from a footbridge kit, especially any leftovers (as buying a full kit for just a few parts would be rather wasteful).

SIGNAL GANTRIES

In some situations, it is not possible to use separate posts for signals, usually because so many signals are required in the same location that it would be confusing to train drivers, or that the posts simply would not fit. When this is the case, signalling engineers install a gantry that spans some or all of the tracks. The necessary signals can then be spaced along the top of the gantry.

The same rules apply to the junction signals on a gantry as when they are on a single post. When semaphore signals are used, the shorter posts indicate the diverging route. If colour light signals are used, fewer signals are required and a feather shows when the signal relates to the diverging route.

While signal gantries are more usually found in very busy railway locations with lots of lines, such as a major station or a complicated junction, you could justify one at a junction or passing loop in a more out-of-the-way location if space at the location modelled was at a premium. In fact, in our model world, physical space often really is at a premium, so a signal gantry may be the only solution on a narrow or short baseboard.

Ratio Plastic Models makes a very realistic kit for a Pratt truss gantry in both OO gauge and N gauge. The prototype would have supported semaphore signals (not included in the kit). Dapol produces a signal gantry kit in OO gauge, which, while not of any particular prototype, represents a typical though sturdily built gantry of the more modern type used for colour light signals. For a purely cosmetic finish, this kit includes mouldings for three-aspect colour light signals.

Scratch-building signal gantries for a specific location or prototype can be a little tricky, since they tend to consist of a truss bridge of some kind. Such structures are quite delicate just to look at, let alone trying to build them using plastic strip, or to cut them out of a piece of card. Plastruct does make lengths of truss girder, which is the hardest part to make, and this would certainly speed up the construction of a signal gantry and improve its robustness.

SEMAPHORE SIGNAL WIRES

Semaphore signals are controlled by wires that connect the arm to the locking frame in a signal box. In some cases, the signals can be quite a distance from the box and the signalman needs to be fairly strong to pull the signal off; returning to danger is easy, since the arm is counterweighted always to return to danger as a safety measure in case the wire breaks.

The signal wire is guided by a series of small pulley wheels. These may be attached to a simple metal bracket that is driven into the ground and several wires can be run one above the other. Alternatively, the pulley wheels may be side by side in a solid iron casting that is fixed to the ground.

Despite the load that can be placed on a signal wire, it is relatively thin stuff, which means that once it is scaled down for a model railway, it may be so thin that it is hardly visible at all. Thicker wire might look better and be more durable on a model, but it might not seem prototypical. Thin cotton might not be thin enough and anyway, cotton has a tendency to fray and attract dust over time. Probably the best material to use is Easiwire, which is often used to represent telegraph wire.

A signal gantry at a junction or place where several signals are required always makes for an impressive structure. This example from Dapol in OO gauge would certainly be an imposing sight on any layout. The three-aspect colour light signal heads are non-working, but it would not be too difficult to substitute working ones.

The simple pulley brackets can be represented with a track pin on which the head is bent through 90 degrees. If you use very thin brass wire (0.33mm or less), this can be soldered to the track pin for rigidity.

To some extent, the infrastructure for signal wires is so slight that it is often easy to miss it in real life. For this reason, few modellers attempt to replicate it on a layout and it is perhaps simplest to omit it.

TURNOUT RODDING

As turnouts can require a bit more strength to move them, turnout rodding is quite a bit more substantial than signal wire. Moving the blades of a turnout or facing turnout lock also requires a bit more mechanical precision, so turnout rodding has greater mechanical complexity.

In a very simple situation where there may be just one or two turnouts for a junction or a passing loop, the absence of turnout rodding on a model would probably not be noticed by most modellers. At more complex junctions, it is common to see so much turnout rodding beside the track that it looks like it should be a walkway. Perhaps the place where an absence of turnout rodding will be most noticeable is in front of a signal box, since this is the point from which all the rodding emanates.

Straight runs of turnout rodding consist of inverted lengths of metal U-section bolted end to end, which are supported in metal brackets that allow the rodding to run on top of rollers.

The view outside a mechanical signal box is perhaps something that Heath Robinson himself would have been proud of. The cranks convert lateral movement through 90 degrees for the turnout rodding, while the wheels do the same for the signal wires (note that chains connect the signal wires around the wheel as friction would snap the wire). Lengths of turnout rodding and signal wire can be seen at the top of the picture along the lineside.
STUART BARDSLEY

In order to go around corners (in reality to cross tracks at 90 degrees), turnout rodding uses right-angled cranks fixed to a base. Where there is more than one length of rodding side by side, the cranks have to be stepped down at different heights so that they do not interfere with each other. The rodding is connected to these lower cranks using an S-shaped piece of rodding called a downset-drive joint. Adjustable cranks are used at the end of a rodding run in order to maintain the necessary level of mechanical precision for the turnout.

Since turnout rodding is metal, it expands in hot weather. To prevent this from altering the mechanical precision of the movement of the turnout, the amount of 'pull' on the rodding needs to equal the amount of 'push', so that the expansion in one cancels out the expansion in the other. Therefore, on long runs of turnout rodding, a compensator is fitted in the middle. This is two cranks joined together that convert pull to push.

All this means that turnout rodding is complex stuff, even when just a couple of turnouts are linked to a signal box or ground frame. Modelling it accurately requires a bit of planning to determine the route that the runs of turnout rodding will take, plus all the necessary cranks and downset-drive joints that will be required.

Simple cosmetic turnout rodding can be constructed using just rectangular plastic strip. The roller guides and cranks can be made using more plastic strip. For ease, the complexities of multiple stepped cranks, downset-drive joints and compensators can all be omitted. Many modellers are quite satisfied just to hint at these items and settle for an impression of turnout rodding rather than absolute fidelity.

If absolute fidelity in OO gauge is what you really want, then you can do no better than to get the turnout-rodding kit made by Wills. All the major turnout-rodding components are included, finely moulded in a suitably coloured grey plastic, which, with a little weathering, will give a realistic finish. An add-on pack of straight rodding is also available for modellers requiring longer runs. Finally, there are likely to be quite a few turnout-rodding components left over and these can be added around a platelayers' hut, in a Signal and Telegraph (S&T) yard, or making up a load in an engineers' wagon.

RELAY CABINETS

A sign of the increasing complexity of the railway infrastructure since the modernization plan has been the growing proliferation of relay cabinets by the lineside. These are used to house electrical equipment

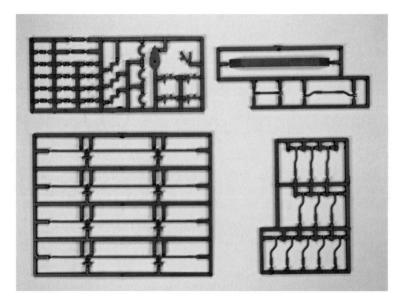

Turnout rodding is quite small when scaled down for a model railway, but packed with all sorts of intricate details, such as supports, expansion links and cranks. Thankfully, if you want to reproduce the look of turnout rodding in OO gauge quite easily, Wills produces a pack with several sprues of very finely moulded parts to cover most basic situations. Just one or two packs should provide sufficient parts for the limited requirements of a siding or passing loop situated between stations.

associated primarily with colour light signals, but also track circuits (for train detection) and the Automatic Warning System (AWS) and its successor, the Train Protection System (TPS).

Relay cabinets are often found next to signals, but they do crop up on their own. They can be in the middle of nowhere, not just near stations with lots of signalling, so they are a great detail to add to any stretch of lineside. They also go hand in hand with the concrete cable trunking used to link signals to signal boxes.

While there are subtle differences between some of the relay cabinets for those who might consider themselves to be 'box spotters', they are essentially just a large metal box with doors on the front. As such, they are easy to scratch-build, since any box structure is quite easy to make from card or plastic strip. It is possible to buy rectangular section from

Relay cabinets are quite common on the modern railway and they come in various shapes and sizes, often differing at the same location, such as here where one has two cupboard doors while the other has just one. The overall faded 'battleship grey' colour is relieved by signs of rust on the left-hand cabinet, while the one on the right has moss growing up the rusting doors. Both have signs proclaiming 'TELECOMS'. While outwardly mundane, they offer opportunities for realistic replication in miniature. STUART BARDSLEY

Plastruct that can form the basis for the tall cabinet structure, simply needing a shallow pitched roof to complete it. The details, such as hinges and door latches, are easily represented with pieces of plastic strip.

Fortunately, modellers who require relay cabinets are well served by kit manufacturers. In N gauge, Ratio Plastic Models makes a set of plastic relay cabinets. In OO gauge, Ten Commandments produces plaster castings of both large and small relay cabinets (note that different-sized relay cabinets are often found grouped together). Wills makes two plastic kits in OO gauge, each for two different styles of relay cabinet, giving four different types in total.

In all cases, all that is required to complete these relay cabinets is a modicum of construction and painting, the latter uniformly being a light 'battleship grey' colour. Installation of the relay cabinets on to a layout is also simple, though they do tend to be mounted on a small concrete base; this is easily represented with a piece of card or plastic sheet painted in a suitable light grey colour and then slightly weathered.

CONCRETE CABLE TRUNKING

Hand in hand with relay cabinets on the modern railway go the miles of concrete cable trunking to be seen by the side of most railway lines. The increasing use of colour light signals and other electrical infrastructure such as track circuits and train detection means that there is a need for cabling to be safely protected. The thin white concrete line by the track, to be glimpsed from the train, houses these myriad cables. The demise of telegraph wires has also seen communication cables moved into cable trunking.

Relay cabinets crop up all over the modern railway, either singly or in groups. These simple OO gauge kits from Wills make an interesting selection of different-sized cabinets for variety. The cabinets are usually finished in an uninspiring shade of 'battleship grey', though this could be livened up with a few rust streaks, especially around the doors.

These relay cabinets are cast in plaster for OO gauge by Ten Commandments. The plaster actually makes a good surface for an interesting paint finish, as its porous nature means that the paint soaks in to different degrees all over. This gives good tonal variation that realistically reflects the way paint finishes weather. The cabinet on the right has had some rust streaks added, although relay cabinets are generally kept in good condition, as the electrical equipment they contain must be kept safe.

Ratio Plastic Models produces a cable trunking kit in N gauge. It might be thought that in this scale it would be hard to notice the trunking or its absence, but the thin grey line is now very much a feature of the modern lineside, even in the smaller scales.

Modellers in OO gauge once again have a choice between products from Ten Commandments and Wills, both being made from injection-moulded plastic. The Wills product is hollow if you actually wanted to put a real cable inside. There is a tab at one end, which makes it easy to slot the sections together. The gaps between each section are moulded all the way around the trough and the lids. Some T-sections are included in order to join the main trunk to the relay cabinets and signals. The trunking is quite wide, as is the case when a lot of cables are to be protected.

The Ten Commandments kit represents a thinner trunking for fewer cables. As well as T-sections, right-angle pieces are included to go around corners. The gaps between the lids are moulded but not the gaps between the actual trough sections, though this will be less noticeable once the trunking has been installed into the track ballast. A very neat detail on this kit is that some of the lids are missing from a couple of sections and the cables inside the trunking can be seen. Indeed, those missing lids are also included so that they can be modelled at the side

of the cable trunking. These displaced lids are quite commonly seen on the real railway.

If you require really long runs of cable trunking as you have a long layout, the commercially available products could be quite expensive to buy in bulk, even though they are excellent products. What is required is to create the impression of cable trunking.

The first option is to use suitably sized plastic strip. This will need notches in the top to represent the separate lid pieces of real trunking. A very fine-bladed saw in a mitre block will allow you to do this. Just a couple of passes with the saw are all that is required, since the gaps between the lids are barely discernible even in real life. You could continue the notches down the sides of the plastic strip, but this is probably a fine detail that is not noticeable once the surrounding area is ballasted. Given that this approach is considered because of the amount of trunking required, it is no small task to add hundreds of notches to the top, never mind the sides.

A quicker approach is to use thick card, at least 2mm thick. Such card can be purchased in art supply shops, while a free supply is the card used at the back of writing pads or in ring-binders. The notches to represent the gaps between the lids can be made using nothing more complicated than a pencil. A very hard leaded pencil such as a 4H is best, since this

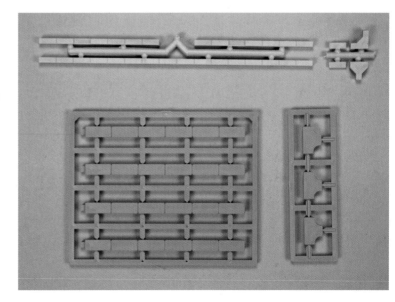

Concrete cable trunking is available for OO gauge in moulded plastic from two manufacturers, namely Ten Commandments (upper) and Wills (lower). Both feature T-junctions to branch off to a relay cabinet. The Ten Commandments product features trunking with the lids missing in places (a common feature on the real lineside) and the lids are even included to place close by. Although both products are moulded in sympathetic 'concrete' colours, both would benefit from painting or matt varnish to remove the plastic finish.

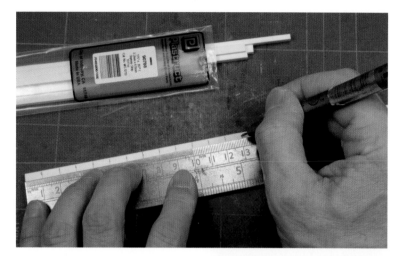

Despite the availability of cable-trunking products, it can be cheaper to make your own if you need a lot. Rectangular plastic strip is ideal and you get quite a bit in one pack. Manufacturers such as Plastruct make plastic strip in a variety of sizes and this pack of 3.2 × 4.8mm (0.125in and 0.187in) strips is ideal for OO gauge. Use a fine-tipped pen to mark every 10mm for the gaps to represent the trunking lids.

RIGHT: The notched effect of the lids can be achieved with a couple of light strokes from a razor saw. Using the saw in a mitre block helps to keep them at right angles. This is enough to mark the plastic strip to suggest where the adjoining edges of the lids are. The real trunking comes as pieces the same length as the lids, so the adjoining edges of this can be represented by also notching sides of the plastic strip.

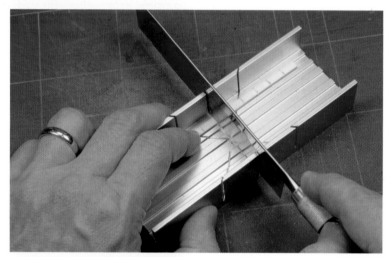

The white plastic needs to be painted a suitable grey concrete colour and then simply installed by the side of the track. Once the ballasting has been done, this simple strip of plastic looks very realistic. The measuring and notching process is simple and quick. It is possible to produce a large amount of trunking in just a couple of hours.

keeps a nice sharp point for thin lines, but with modest pressure it will easily 'score' the card to represent the gaps.

You could cut the card into strips then add the gaps for the lids, but it would be fiddly using a pencil on such thin strips. Far better and quicker is to draw the gaps on to the single sheet of card, then cut it into strips. A couple of A4 sheets of card would provide enough trunking for even the largest layout. All that is needed to complete the job is to paint the strips a suitable concrete colour and install them on the layout.

Although plastic strip is a relatively cheap means of producing a lot of cable trunking, a piece of scrap card is usually even cheaper (and often free). Thick card (about 2mm) is best. Use a sharp pencil and a steel ruler to draw parallel lines that are about 4mm apart for OO gauge. These lines will represent the actual strips of cable trunking.

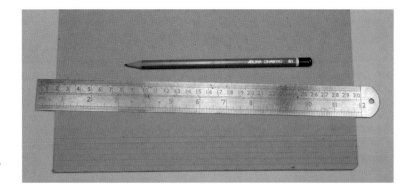

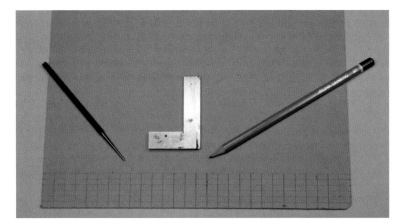

LEFT: The adjoining edges of the trunking lids can now be added 10mm apart (for OO gauge). There are two methods. On the left, a scriber has been used to add shallow grooves to the cardboard. This has to be done carefully to avoid scratching the cardboard, as the fibrous nature of the material will then give 'fluffy' edges. On the right, a very hard draughtsman's pencil (a 4H) has been used to draw the lines. The hard pencil is slightly better at scoring the cardboard.

Cardboard of a suitable grey concrete colour does not need painting as it is not shiny like plastic. In this view, it has been painted a light grey as the cardboard was too dark in colour. The fibrous nature of cardboard lends the cable trunking a slightly rough texture, just like real concrete.

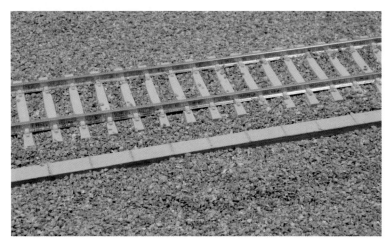

CHAPTER SEVEN

MISCELLANEOUS LINESIDE DETAILS

There is a wide range of miscellaneous details that can be included in a model railway's representation of the lineside. Many of these details are signs, either to warn people or to give information to train drivers. Some details are there to describe the railway's vast infrastructure, such as mileposts and gradient signs.

Rubbish is an unwelcome detail in real life, as is graffiti, while telegraph poles are a detail that is firmly evocative of the steam era. Finally, if you have a sense of humour and perhaps want to see yourself on your own model railway, you can include some train spotters eagerly admiring your locomotive collection.

SIGNS

Railways have always been generous with their signage. While lineside fencing is designed to keep people out, it does not do any harm to remind people not to climb over it. At unguarded crossings, signs exist to warn people of the dangers that trains present. A lot of signs are informational and many exist for the benefit of railway personnel, such as speed signs in order to help them with the safe and efficient running of the railway.

WARNING SIGNS

The use of signs to warn both the public and railway employees goes back to the earliest days of the railways and continues to this day. The style of the signs might have changed and how they are made, but the objective is the same – to warn people of danger in order to protect them. Railways can be dangerous places and the public and sometimes the employees need to be reminded.

As with so many lineside details, the steam era railway companies had their own styles of signage and language, such that it is often possible to tell the railway company to which the sign belonged just by looking at it. The language tended towards the

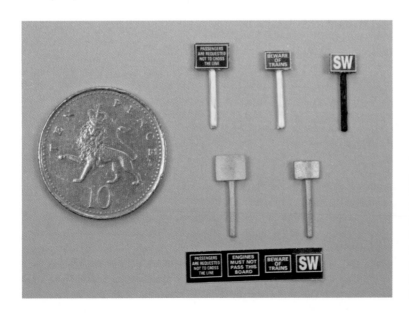

These diminutive N-gauge signs produced by P&D Marsh are cast in white metal with printed fronts to be cut out and glued on. Unpainted examples are shown (lower) with three finished signs (upper). They require no great modelling skills to complete them. The text is quite legible, though probably not from normal viewing distance.

verbose and some signs contained so many words that you wonder that anybody ever bothered to read right to the end, especially in an age when illiteracy was still not that uncommon.

These signs were initially cast in iron from wooden patterns, thus were solid yet durable. The letters were picked out in white against a contrasting background such as black or red; you can tell that these signs were made in an age when labour was cheap and plentiful. Later on, with the spread of advertising, some warning signs were produced in the same way, enamelled on to tin plate. Modern signage is much more efficiently printed on to steel sheets, often with a reflective background to assist in seeing the signs at night.

Some warning signs are available in model form, such as those produced for OO gauge by Tiny Signs. These simply require cutting out, then fixing to a wall or a post. The latter is easily made from plastic rod or a piece of thick wire to which the sign can be glued. If the sign is going to be mounted on a post, remember to colour the rear of the sign, as this will just be white card; a felt-tip pen is ideal. If the sign does not have a white border, use a felt-tip pen to colour the edges as well.

CREATING YOUR OWN SIGNS

If you are comfortable using a personal computer and word-processing software, it is quite simple to create your own signs to print off yourself. Hundreds of different fonts are available, so it is usually possible to find a suitable one to represent a specific sign or railway company. Most word-processing software allows the creation of borders around the text if required, as well as white text on a black background (or any other colour combination).

Having created your own artwork for a sign, it is possible to size it to whatever dimensions you require, usually as small as it goes. Then you can send it to your printer. A laser printer gives the best reproduction, though most people have ink-jet printers. All printers work by forming the image from little dots applied to the paper. The better the printer, the smaller those dots will be and it will be able to get more dots into a given space.

A problem can be that many home-use printers simply cannot print text small enough to make a scale railway warning sign. The results are often fuzzy, indistinguishable letters or pixilation whereby curves seem jagged and indistinct. One solution is to print the sign at a size that the printer can handle, be it twice or even ten times the required size. The resulting image can be reduced (often several times) on a photocopier until it is the desired size. Good-quality photocopiers can be found in office supply shops and libraries and the charge to use them is often quite reasonable.

There are many examples of original warning signs to be found, often on display at preserved railways. If you can track down the sign that you want, it is a simple matter to photograph it and get it printed. With digital images these days it is possible to resize the photograph to the dimensions required for the model.

When printed on to proper photographic paper, a much better resolution is possible than even the best home printer can achieve. Avoid the 'print them yourself' machines in some shops as these are basically just a laser printer; the prints are good, but not as good as when proper photographic paper is used. Given the superior print quality of photographs, you can even copy text from a word processer to a digital-image file, change the dimensions to those required, then have it printed in superior quality on photographic paper. Bear in mind that if you have exact dimensions for the model in your image file, photographic printers specify a margin of 1 or 2 per cent difference on the actual print.

Remember that even in O gauge, a lot of the writing on a typical warning sign can be too small to read with the naked eye, even close up, never mind from normal viewing distance. What matters then is giving the correct impression of a sign. Lines of white 'dots and dashes' on a piece of black card may be all that is required. Few of us carry around a magnifying glass actually to read the minute model signs, though for many modellers it is important to know that the detail is there even if you cannot actually see it.

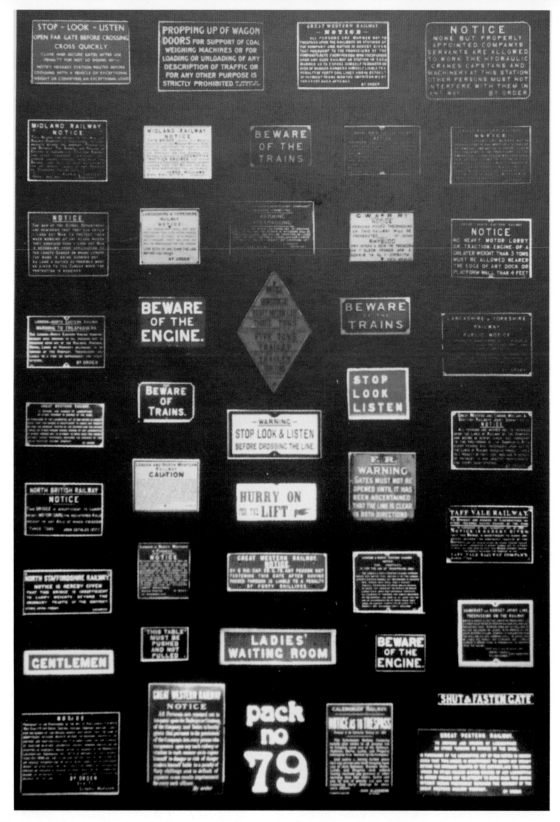

Tiny Signs (now produced by Gaugemaster) produces a sheet of general signs for OO gauge, including lineside warning signs. For example, a Furness Railway sign reads 'Warning – gates must not be opened until it has been ascertained that the line is clear in both directions'. The signs are printed on card and are easily cut out and attached to a wall, a fence or a post.

This sign was photographed on the end of a platform at Warrington Bank Quay station. It is full of character, showing as it does the signs of wear, weather and vandalism. The font of the late British Rail era is available for home computers and you could recreate the sign yourself; however, a quicker method is to use the photograph itself as the basis for a warning sign.

RIGHT: The original photograph was taken from a slightly elevated angle. This leads to a distorted image, in that the corners of the sign are no longer perfect right angles. When taking a photograph of a real sign, try to stand with the camera pointing straight at the sign in order to avoid this. However, with a basic mastery of photo-editing software, it is quite easy to rectify the distortion as well as correcting the colour, brightness and contrast of the image.

Once you are happy with the image of the sign, resize it so that it is suitable for your chosen modelling scale, in this case OO gauge (the same as the figure). Print it out and stick it to some thin card to give it strength. A suitable pole is easily fashioned from a piece of wire. The finished sign looks just like the real thing, though it does illustrate that all but the largest text is illegible and that, unless viewed close up, even that will be hard to see.

SPEED SIGNS

As for motorists on the roads, railways use speed signs to indicate to train drivers the maximum permissible (and hence safe) speed on a section of track. Speed restrictions may be in place for a number of reasons, for example on very tight corners where speed could lead to a derailment, or at junctions where similarly an excess of speed could cause an accident while travelling through the turnouts.

Modern speed signs usually consist of large metal numerals atop a metal pole. The numbers are painted yellow for visibility and the poles are painted black. Some feature a yellow painted arrow that points to left or right; these are used at turnouts to indicate the maximum speed on the diverging (that is, curved) part of the turnout.

Ten Commandments makes a fret of N gauge speed signs laser-cut into thin black card. All that is required is to separate them carefully from the fret and paint the numerals yellow. Paint is fine, although there is a risk of gunging up the fine numerals in this small scale unless the paint is heavily thinned. An alternative is a yellow pencil or fine felt-tip pen of the kind used by artists. The thin card poles can be planted into a suitable hole drilled into the baseboard, but they are likely to be very susceptible to damage. If greater robustness is required, it is a simple job to add a piece of 0.5mm brass wire to the back of the card pole, which will give greater rigidity and strength.

You could make your own speed signs, especially in the larger scales. Plastic alphabets of differing sizes are available from Plastruct that are easily mounted on to a pole made from plastic rod. Fretting out your own numerals could be tricky, though you could compromise by printing them on to card.

The most modern speed signs closely resemble road signs, being a black numeral on a white background mounted on a round plate edged with red. Such signs are easily constructed on a computer and, since they are larger than warning signs, most home printers should be able to cope with printing a quality finish. Glossy photographic paper would provide a hint of the reflective nature of these modern signs, although a coat of gloss varnish on paper will achieve the same result.

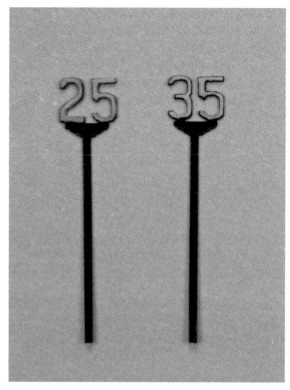

Ten Commandments produces a superb set of modern era speeds signs in N gauge that simply require the numerals to be painted yellow. The thin card used can be planted in a hole in the baseboard, but this will be liable to damage. Therefore, it is advisable to back the pole with 0.5mm brass wire, which will be strong enough and flexible enough to withstand accidental knocks.

GRADIENT SIGNS

Railways prefer to run on the flat, as going up hills requires more effort and even coming down them can also be a nuisance if all the brakes need to be pinned down on an unfitted steam era goods train. But Britain is not flat and, despite the best efforts of the Victorian railway engineers, most railway routes have some gradients on them. It is important that train drivers know about these gradients so that they can control the locomotive accordingly. This was more of an issue in the steam era, so that was when you would most commonly see gradient signs.

Gradient signs were quite characteristic, being two arms either side of a central post. They were usually placed where the gradient changed significantly, say from the flat to the slope, in which case one arm would be horizontal for the flat and the other would be at an angle corresponding to the slope (either up or down). The angle of the sloping arm was more indicative than precisely measured to a minute degree. The actual gradient was written on the arm, usually black letters on a white background.

Hornby has produced plastic gradient signs for many years and these tend to be still available as part of a pack of lineside equipment. They are typical of the type of gradient sign used in the steam era and sometimes still seen by the lineside to this day.

Whatever scale you model in, a gradient sign is quite easy to make. The post and arms can be made from sections of plastic strip of the relevant size. The lettering on the arms can be prepared on a computer and printed off on to white paper, which can then be cut out and glued to the arms. It is possible to get thin white card through some home printers. This offers the possibility of drawing the whole shape of the gradient sign and the lettering using a computer.

Once printed, the shape can be cut out using a sharp craft knife.

WHISTLE SIGNS

Train drivers know to sound the whistle (or horn) in certain obvious places where the approach of their train may be obscured to track gangs by, for example, a bridge. Some instances where a warning needs to be given are less obvious, such as approaching an unguarded crossing, particularly if it is obscured by the curvature of the line. To inform drivers when they need to sound a warning, railway companies installed 'whistle' signs an appropriate distance before the site of the potential hazard.

Some signs literally spelt out 'whistle', while others were abbreviated to 'SW' for 'sound whistle'. Hornby has made a whistle sign for many years, but, once again, such signs are easily made by the modeller using a sign created on a computer and printed at home. The support for the sign can be made from plastic strip.

At first sight, these OO gauge gradient signs and mileposts from Hornby appear a little toy-like. By cutting off the prominent plastic bases, the signs will look much better. Alternatively, the bases could be covered by the scenic ground cover on the layout. Finally, a coat of matt varnish will tone down their obviously plastic appearance.

Gradient signs are easy enough to make from plastic card, or they can be cut out from card as one piece. This example uses Plastruct plastic strip, namely square section for the post and thin rectangular strip for the arms. The writing has been prepared on a computer and then printed to the required size. The printout is simply cut out and glued to the arms. Note that the post is overlong as it will be 'planted' into a hole in the baseboard.

RIGHT: It is important for train drivers to know when they need to sound the whistle (or horn) for something that they may not be able to see, such as round a corner or beyond a bridge. Such warnings are vital for unmanned crossings. This OO gauge sign is made by Hornby. The prominent plastic base can be hidden by scenery, the resulting sign being a small but realistic detail for the lineside.

These modern era whistle signs are laser-cut into thin card in N gauge by Ten Commandments. They simply need the letters to be painted white (a paint pen is ideal for this delicate job). A piece of 0.5mm brass wire is advisable behind the post to prevent damage. Signs such as this are easy to scratch-build in any scale, especially if you can find the correct-sized letters in plastic, such as those produced by Plastruct.

A 'whistle' sign is easy to make in any scale. This example uses Plastruct square section for posts and a piece of plastic sheet for the actual sign. The word 'whistle' has been printed using a computer, so it just needs cutting out and gluing on. Double-sided sticky tape is ideal for this, as other glues may cause the thin plastic sheet to bow as the glue dries.

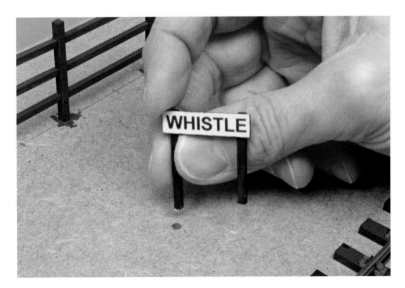

The whistle sign deliberately has one post longer than the other. This is to make it easy to 'plant' it on to the layout. The Plastruct square section is 2.5mm square and some simple geometry reveals that a 3.5mm hole will be a perfect fit for this. With care, an interference fit is possible, though make sure to drill the hole as close to 90 degrees from the vertical as possible.

MILEPOSTS

Mileposts were originally found on roads to supply simple information to travellers and they were later adopted by the canals so that boats knew where they were in relation to where they were going. Not surprisingly, the railways installed mileposts as well. Initially, this was for the benefit of passengers, so that they could confirm that they had indeed travelled the distance for which they had paid. Eventually, the milepost was more for those who worked on and maintained the railway (though those whose hobby is the recording of time trials will no doubt appreciate the presence of mileposts as an essential part of the calculation).

Mileposts were not actually found every mile, since the Railways' Clauses Act of 1845 stipulated that they should be placed every quarter of a mile. Thus the intermediate posts would display the number of miles and the intermediate value (quarter, half or three quarters).

Once again, the style of mileposts could be distinctive dependent upon the railway company that made them. They could range from simple wooden posts or stones with the numbers painted on, to more robust cast-iron mileposts with two faces that allowed the number to be clearly seen from either direction.

The plastic mileposts made by Hornby represent the double-faced type; they are possibly a little chunky and over-scale for OO gauge, but there is no reason why they could not be used in O gauge instead.

Scratch-building your own mileposts is quite easy, since they can be as simple as you wish them to be. A number printed on a computer or obtained from a set of transfers is easily applied to a simple post. If you have a decent length of lineside available, you may even be able to place the mileposts a scale distance apart, although selective compression would allow you to place them closer if necessary.

While many mileposts remain, the march of modernization, such as the move towards the European Rail Traffic Management System, will sound the death knell for the humble milepost. The contemporary railway has measured in metric for many years and, very soon, the mileposts will be replaced with new location markers every kilometre or half-kilometre.

TELEGRAPH POLES

Now that the modern railway stows all its cabling in concrete trunking, it is difficult to imagine that hardly any railway route in the steam era would have been unaccompanied along its length by the regularly spaced sentinels of the telegraph pole.

The railways were early adopters of not just revolutionary mechanical technology, but also ground-breaking electrical equipment. The telegraph and then the telephone allowed signal boxes to communicate as part of the safe operation of the block working system and generally for the railways to operate effectively without recourse to slow and cumbersome paper-based communication. To support this network of communication, the telegraph wires followed the railway wherever it went.

Telegraph poles are just poles, so the main differences relate to the number of wires that needed to be carried. On a lightly used branch line, there might be just a few wires, therefore a few arms each with an insulator would suffice. The poles on major main lines

These telegraph poles are produced in N gauge by Kestrel Designs. Although moulded in black, there are two reasons for painting them. Firstly, creosoted poles are not perfectly black, more shades of brown and black. Secondly, the shiny plastic looks unrealistic. The insulators then need painting white. Considering the smaller scale, there is very good detail on these telegraph poles, such as the steps near the top for the linesman.

would carry far more wires, such that the poles were festooned with arms each with multiple insulators. When things got extremely busy, two poles might be placed side by side in order to support much longer arms capable of supporting more insulators. Some telegraph poles would be supported by an additional angled pole if there was a risk of the pole toppling, for example on the side of a steep cutting.

In N gauge, Kestrel Designs produce a set of ready-to-plant telegraph poles. These are moulded in black plastic and just need to be planted into pre-drilled holes. Being plastic, they would benefit from a coat of paint to represent the creosote finish that is typical of the steam era.

The 'sleeper grime' brown paints sold for painting sleepers are ideal, as sleepers were similarly creosoted. To speed things up, consider buying an aerosol of this paint; simply stick all the poles into a piece of polystyrene to hold them up and they can be painted in just a few seconds. A finishing touch is to paint the insulators white; being ceramic, this is the colour they would have been and a few blobs of colour help to lift the otherwise drab appearance of a telegraph pole.

Peco produces some very fine telegraph poles for O gauge. Ratio Plastic Models produces ready-to-plant

telegraph poles in both N gauge and OO gauge and the same comments apply as for the Kestrel Designs product. Model Scene Accessories also makes ready-to-plant telegraph poles. Once again, they are moulded in brown plastic, but this time the insulators have been painted white for the modeller. These poles come with a round base, so no holes are required to be drilled in the baseboard to plant them.

While they will stand up on their own, the bases are not at all prototypical. There are two options. The first is simply to cut the bases off and plant the poles into holes in the baseboard. The second option is to glue the poles to the baseboards and disguise the bases. This can be done by building up the scenery around the base using either thick card or a skim of filler. Once all the scenic work is complete and scatter materials have been added, the base will not be visible.

Dapol still manufactures the old Kitmaster telegraph poles from many years ago. There is the added bonus of a couple of cable drums as well, which can be left at the lineside where maintenance work is in progress. These poles are moulded in Dapol's standard light grey plastic, so they will definitely need painting. They have optional bases, so you can either

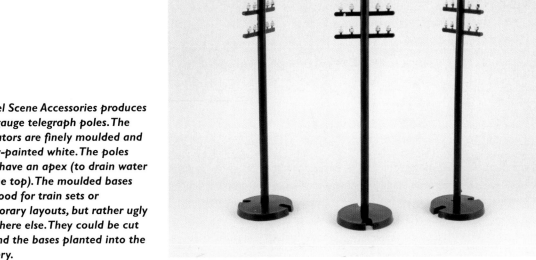

Model Scene Accessories produces OO gauge telegraph poles. The insulators are finely moulded and ready-painted white. The poles even have an apex (to drain water off the top). The moulded bases are good for train sets or temporary layouts, but rather ugly anywhere else. They could be cut off and the bases planted into the scenery.

If you fix the Model Scene Accessories telegraph poles to the layout before you do any scenic work, it is quite easy to hide the plastic bases. Simply smooth some filler around the base of the pole. Any kind of filler will do, but do not apply it too thickly or it may crack as it dries; several thin layers are better.

RIGHT: **Once the scatter materials have been added, it is impossible to see the plastic base used on the Model Scene Accessories telegraph poles. This may seem like a lot of effort when you could just cut the bases off and plant the poles into holes in the scenery; however, by retaining the bases, the poles will be exceptionally robust against accidental damage, especially as the poles are made from flexible plastic.**

plant the poles into holes, or use the bases to make it easier to get them to stand up. These bases have a representation of random ground cover, unlike the smooth bases of the Model Scene Accessories product. Suitably painted, they will need less effort to blend them into the scenery.

The Dapol telegraph poles require one arm to be glued to the pole and the kit includes a choice of arms with four, two or one insulator, so you can customize your telegraph poles to an extent. It is worth noting that you can take any of these manufacturers' telegraph poles and remove some of the insulators

Dapol produces the old Kitmaster telegraph poles in OO gauge. The grey plastic needs to be painted, so an aerosol or an airbrush can speed things up if you need a lot of telegraph poles. These kits have an optional base that can be disguised, or you can just plant the poles directly into the scenery. In addition, there are parts to make some cable drums.

or some of the arms for, say, a branch line that needs fewer wires along the line.

Having planted your telegraph poles along the lineside, there is the thorny issue of whether or not to have some representation of the telegraph wires themselves, and how best to recreate them. Even modest telegraph poles can have upwards of a dozen wires strung between them. While the wires in real life are thin, the fact that so many are grouped together in close proximity means that they are quite prominent. While the easiest option is to omit the wires, the fact that they are missing may stand out like a sore thumb.

Telegraph wires are difficult to model, not least because the real wires drooped between two poles. Looking out of the window on a train journey would often provide the 'up-down, up-down' rhythm of watching the telegraph wires. This droop between poles is hard to replicate, since you cannot scale down the weight of real wire and let gravity do the rest.

If using the thinnest possible black cotton to represent the wire, it tends to curl rather than droop thanks to the way it was wound and stored on the bobbin. For this reason, modellers who do include the wires tend to pull them tight between the insulators. This at least ensures that the model wires are not curling out of control. You can wrap cotton around the insulator and secure it with a spot of clear-drying superglue. Be careful not to tighten the cotton too much between poles, or they may end up bending. It is also worth noting that the poles need to be firmly anchored into the scenery, as they have to maintain a modicum of tension in order to keep the model wires straight.

Cotton is a cheap and simple source for the wires, but it has some drawbacks. It can fray over time and it seems to attract and display dust and stray hairs more than you would expect. Some modellers use fishing line, but this tends to be white rather than black. The best product is an American one called EZ Line. This is green in colour, but this is not so bad as copper wires would oxidize to a green colour over time. Best of all, EZ Line has a little bit of elasticity to it, which makes it more forgiving both when you tension it to begin with and if you should accidentally catch the wires with your hand.

Scratch-building telegraph poles is fairly simple, since the necessary poles and arms can be represented with plastic strip, such as the range produced by Plastruct. If you wanted really tough telegraph poles to stand up to modest punishment such as may be received on a portable layout, you could solder together brass rod and strip. Given the range of more than adequate telegraph poles available from manufacturers, there is probably not much point scratch-building telegraph poles unless you want, for example, particularly tall ones (to clear a bridge).

RUBBISH

You might think that treating the railway line as a convenient dumping ground is a modern problem, but this is not the case. The lineside boundary fence that keeps the rest of the world off railway property has always been an irresistible temptation when someone has an unwanted item to dispose of. Sadly, people seem content to believe that once the rubbish is over the fence, it is someone else's problem.

The inclusion or otherwise of rubbish on your model railway is a purely personal choice. Many

It is hard to imagine in this age of wireless communication and fast fibre-optic cabling just how much the railways relied on telegraph wires to operate. In some places there were so many wires that twin-pole telegraph poles were utilized. This example is from Hornby. It comes with a rather obtrusive connector that plugs into Hornby's own track in order to position the poles correctly by the lineside.

modellers like to craft their model railway layout with rose-tinted spectacles, recreating a time and place that is perceived or perhaps remembered to be better than the here and now. Such models have no place for rubbish to spoil the illusion. At the other extreme, some modellers love the challenge of recreating a time and place as it really was, warts and all. So if rubbish is a part of that reality, they have to include it in model form.

Anything and everything can become rubbish, simply by the act of no longer wanting it and carelessly throwing it away. This means that some rubbish is small while some is big and with everything in-between. Small items of rubbish might be drinks cans and fast-food packaging. As these are small in real life, once they are scaled down to model size they can be so small as to be virtually unseen. Only where they collect en masse do you really notice them. Modelling discarded N gauge beer cans might just be possible with very thin plastic rod, but painting them different colours for variety would test even the greatest patience.

Newspaper tends to get everywhere, though thankfully it does rot down eventually. This is an easier prospect for modelling, since the wind-blown pages of a tabloid or broadsheet are big enough to see and model in a small scale. Actual newspaper is probably the best material to use as it is quite a thin paper and therefore easily scrunched and distressed. You can cut newspaper into little rectangles, then pick different pages for a variety of colours. Best of all is to use a cross-cut shredder, since one of these will quickly produce enough newspaper rubbish for a hundred layouts.

Next up on the scale of rubbish comes household items. A roll of carpet is easy to produce by just rolling up a piece of paper. White goods such as washing machines and freezers can easily be made up from white card, since from normal viewing distance they are just white boxes and a few dents and creases would add to the realism, especially for items that have had a hefty fall down an embankment. Pieces of furniture such as a sofa are a bit more tricky, as they are more shapely than just a box, but pieces of card can easily be made to form an impression of a sofa. A mattress from a bed is quite easy, as it just requires a rectangle from a piece of thick card. A huge help for all of these items is to use the downloadable PDF file from Scalescenes.

At the top end of the rubbish scale are really big items, the biggest of which is probably a car. Usually this is a stolen car that ends up being dumped and set on fire. No company produces a model of a burnt-out car, but the vast range of ready-made model cars from the likes of Oxford Diecast is so cheap that you can afford to buy a showroom-finish model and vandalize it yourself. The first thing is to pull the tyres off. Disassembly of the body will make it easier to remove the glazing, usually by drilling out the rivets that hold the body to the chassis.

It is sadly a feature of modern times that some people regard the railway lineside as a convenient receptacle for all kinds of unwanted items. If you really want to embrace gritty reality for your model railway, you can do no better than these washing machines, cookers, sofas, mattresses and carpets. Produced by Scalescenes for OO gauge and N gauge (the former illustrated here), they come as a PDF that you can print out as many times as you want. They are simple to make up with laminations of card to support the paper exteriors.

An abandoned car by the lineside makes an interesting scenic detail. The starting point for this project is an OO gauge Morris Marina made by Oxford Diecast. Out of the box, the model is in 'showroom condition'; it might seem a shame to vandalize such a nice model, but as they can be purchased for just a few pounds you do not need to worry about destroying it.

The first step is to disassemble the model. A cross-headed jeweller's screwdriver is all that is needed to remove two screws that hold everything together. Some models, especially older ones, are riveted together and if that is the case it is necessary carefully to drill out the rivets.

With the screws removed, the model literally collapses into its component parts. Keep the small screws safe for reassembly later on. The glazing is not required, so this can be discarded. For an extra level of vandalism, the wheels can be removed. These simply pull off the axles. The axles are then loose, so they need to be glued in place.

The showroom-condition paintwork on the body needs to be severely distressed to represent an abandoned or burnt-out car. Simply use a glass-fibre burnishing brush to rub off the glossy finish on the paint. Make sure that you wear disposable rubber gloves, as the stray fibres from the burnishing brush can be an annoying irritant.

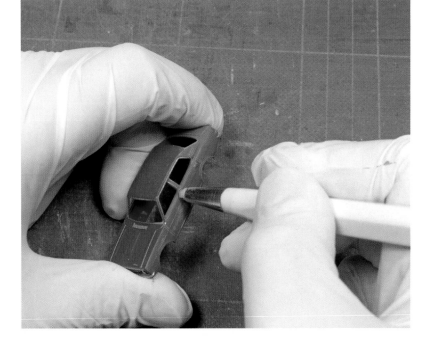

ABOVE: *After distressing with a glass-fibre burnishing brush, the car looks more like it has had a hard life before abandonment. In some places, the paint has been removed down to bare metal. For an abandoned car, this level of distressing would probably be sufficient, but a burnt-out car needs more work.*

LEFT: *The heat of a burning car tends to blister the paintwork. This can be represented by using a suitable rust-coloured paint and some weathering powder. Some of the powder is mixed into a bit of the paint on a palette and then stippled on to areas of the car.*

RIGHT: The battered and distressed paintwork can be further toned down using washes of rust-coloured paints. A wash in this case uses very thin paint to wash over the model. The Humbrol Rust Wash enamel is heavily thinned already, while acrylics can be easily thinned with nothing more than water.

BELOW: The completed car is reassembled by screwing the chassis and seat mouldings back on to the body. This windowless rusting hulk is now a shadow of its former self. Once it is planted on to a layout and surrounded with some weeds and other rubbish, it will look like it has been abandoned, set alight and then left to rot.

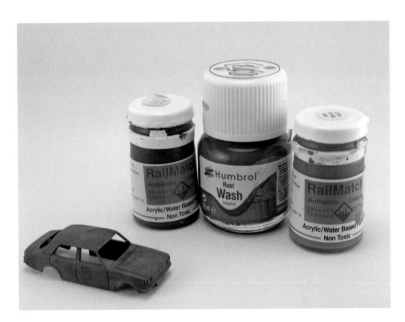

It is probably inadvisable actually to set fire to the model and it would not give a realistic effect anyway. The main thing is to distress the glossy paintwork, which can be done with a glass-fibre burnishing brush. Then various washes of rust colour and black can be used to give the effect of blistering and damage caused by the heat of a fire. The completed model would certainly look unusual by the lineside of a modern era layout.

Not all of the rubbish to be found by the lineside is the result of antisocial behaviour; the railways are responsible for quite a bit of rubbish themselves (though they usually clean it up eventually). Most of this unwanted material is the result of maintenance

A pile of bricks makes for an unassuming lineside feature, perhaps where something has been demolished, such as an old platelayers' hut. Individual bricks would be tediously difficult to model in any scale in sufficient quantity to make a pile. Therefore, it comes as a relief to OO gauge modellers that Harburn Hobbies sells a ready-to-plant pile of bricks.

or clearance work. Piles of old sleepers and lengths of rail can often be seen strewn by the lineside. Old buildings such as platelayers' huts and signal boxes get demolished and leave behind a pile of bricks or scraps of wood.

All of these things are easy to model; even a pile of bricks is conveniently available as a pre-coloured one-piece casting from Harburn Hobbies. Scraps of buildings can be made from any spare parts or off-cuts left over from completing a kit; the old adage of 'never throw anything away because it may be useful' is especially true for railway modellers.

GRAFFITI

Love it or loathe it, graffiti is a fact of modern life, but its inclusion on a model railway, like rubbish, is purely a matter of personal taste. Including graffiti on a model portrays the gritty realism of modern life,

although some modellers feel that this somehow legitimizes what is essentially an act of vandalism and thus choose to avoid modelling it. Graffiti ranges from the banality of 'Kilroy was here' all the way to vast colourful expressions that would be works of art if they were not sprayed on to a railway retaining wall.

The application of simple graffiti consisting of words and names is very easy to do and requires little more that painting the letters by hand with white paint. For a bit of variety you could use thinned white paint which has a tendency to run, leaving a few streaks down the wall.

The more complex multicoloured graffiti is harder to do by hand unless you are quite artistic and capable with a paintbrush. Fortunately, waterslide transfers of graffiti are available. Some of these are American products intended for railway 'boxcars', which are heavily targeted in that country in real

Before the age of graffiti as a 'work of art', it tended to be no more than simple slogans daubed on with a paintbrush. Football teams and 'Kilroy' were prevalent. This is easily achieved with a modeller's paintbrush, or, better still, a white pencil or a paint pen. Remember to keep the size of letters in context to the scale, certainly no bigger than about half the size of a model figure, as in this OO gauge example. Graffiti should appear at the bottom of tall walls, as vandals are unlikely to be carrying stepladders with them.

life. Fortunately (or not), graffiti is international and needs no translation, so these products are becoming increasingly popular on this side of the Atlantic. Waterslide transfers are simple to apply and they form easily over details such as embossed brickwork.

TRAINSPOTTERS

No lineside is complete without some train enthusiasts somewhere along the length of a railway route. Trainspotters are generally to be found in their natural habitat of a station, although not exclusively so. There is no reason why some enthusiasts should not be on some stretch of the lineside, either schoolboys on their way home, or grown-up enthusiasts looking for a good location at which to take down numbers or to get a good photograph.

Any model figure stood by the lineside could be said to be an enthusiast, or at the very least someone just watching the trains go by. Two types of figure really say 'trainspotter' and each is indicative of its respective era.

For many schoolboys in the steam era, the purchase of an Ian Allan 'ABC' book and the underlining of the numbers it contained was the ultimate hobby. It was very much a post-war phenomenon and so modellers should limit it to the nationalized British Railways era. Bachmann Scenecraft produces a set of six trainspotter figures in OO gauge, four of whom are schoolboys. These are exquisitely moulded and painted model figures and they would look superb grouped by a lineside fence or on a footbridge.

The invention of the aerosol can has sadly been a boon for graffiti 'artists'. The results are complex and colourful. You can paint or draw your own, but there are a number of sheets of transfers of graffiti such as these examples from Ancorton Models. However, many transfer sheets are not created using a printer capable of printing white, just thin colours on a transfer paper. This means that they work best on very light-coloured backgrounds.

In the modern era, taking down numbers is still a popular pastime. The advent of cheaper cameras and film means that more and more enthusiasts of all ages are able to record not just the numbers, but a photograph of the railway scene. The digital revolution and even today's relatively cheap digital cameras (or never mind the camera, just use your mobile phone) mean that enthusiasts at the lineside are more likely to be using a camera than a pencil and notebook.

The German company Preiser produces a set of six camera-wielding enthusiasts. Although to the scale of HO (which is subtly smaller than OO gauge), as real people come in all shapes and sizes the difference in scale will be impossible to see, so these figures will be quite at home on a British-based layout. As with all the figures produced by Preiser, these train enthusiasts are well moulded and beautifully painted.

So whatever era you model, why not include a few trainspotters by the lineside? Let your imagination pretend that it is really you down there by the lineside, reliving the old days, or just simply enjoying your model railway layout creation.

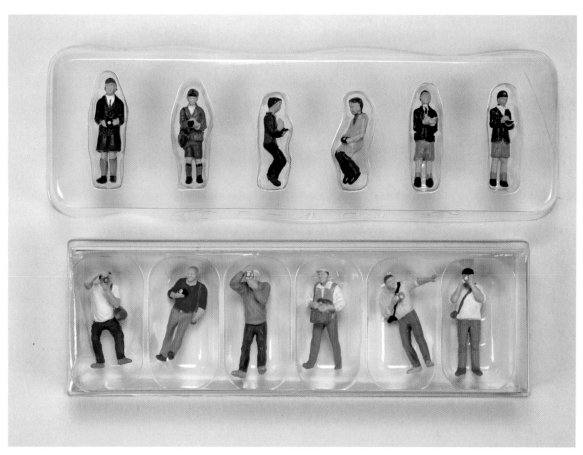

What lineside scene would be complete without a few trainspotters to remind you of your own youth? The upper pack of ready-painted figures in OO gauge is from Bachmann Scenecraft, mostly representing steam era schoolboys complete with Ian Allan 'ABCs'. The lower pack is from Preiser and the schoolboys are generally more modern because they have cameras, although they would still look acceptable in scenes from the late 1950s onwards.

CHAPTER EIGHT

BRINGING IT ALL TOGETHER

Thus far the chapters in this book have looked at all the different elements that can be found at the lineside. Most of them can be seen in isolation, but it is more common to find several of them grouped together. For example, a level crossing might be found near to a signal box and a signal box will certainly be found where there are signals.

The trick to achieving a great effect when modelling a section of railway and its associated lineside is to know how to blend the different elements together. The first thing is not to overdo it. It might be tempting to cram everything into a scene, especially if you only have room for a short stretch of lineside between stations. Remember the adage that 'less is more'. If you really are stuck for space, just pick a few of the lineside elements that you want the most.

By choosing to forgo a station to maximize the length of the lineside that can be modelled, all the lineside elements that interest you can be included. If you have a reasonable amount of space, you can spread a selection of features out across the lineside that you are modelling. Remember, though, that the vast majority of real lineside is actually quite feature-less. There will be fencing and if it is the steam era there will be telegraph poles. Yet the instances of signal boxes, level crossings, platelayers' huts and so on will be small in real life. A realistic lineside scene will need to be a balance between having the features that interest you and the likely occurrence of these features in any given stretch of railway line.

This chapter includes some examples of lineside scenes using the elements that are described in this book. Each one has been made as a diorama rather than a layout, but they show what you can achieve. You can follow them slavishly, or adapt them to your own particular layout requirements. They are all examples of how you can model the lineside.

A DETAILED PLATELAYERS' HUT

This scene has been modelled in O gauge in order to maximize the possibilities for fine detail that this larger scale provides. Few modellers have enough space for an O gauge layout at home (though most model railway clubs have a reasonably sized O gauge layout). This restriction on space means that most home-based O gauge layouts are of the simple terminus type, since the space needed for the curves to make an oval layout would require a large room.

Given the restrictions on space, it is likely that there will be limited opportunity to model the lineside in all its vast, open main line form. More likely is a very short stretch of railway line between a terminus station and a fiddle yard. In this case, it is quality that counts over quantity.

Therefore, this scene uses a platelayers' hut as its focal point and develops a scene around it. It can be quite compact and the scene modelled in this example is contained within a length of just 457mm (18in), which is quite a modest space for the larger scale. Of course, there is no reason why this philosophy cannot be used in the smaller scales as well if you are really stuck for space.

The centrepiece is the Peco kit for a brick-built platelayers' hut. This is just one of several similarly sized huts that are available in O gauge. They have enough presence on a model in O gauge to be the central feature without overwhelming the space available.

The scene can be expanded with various associated elements, such as the piles of sleepers and ballast bin produced by Ten Commandments. These items would naturally be found by a platelayers' hut, so they logically develop the scene. The fencing at the rear of the scene uses scratch-built items; commercial products are available, but it can be cheaper to make your own and not too time-consuming for such a relatively short stretch of lineside.

One of the major advantages of O gauge is that its greater size gives modellers the opportunity to include much higher levels of detail. A detail pack is available from Peco that includes various platelayers' tools. Other details such as the lineside signs have been scratch-built. Such details really bring the scene alive. They encourage the eye to linger on the scene and therefore discourage the brain from recognizing that the area of lineside modelled is actually very small.

Before jumping in, it is worth mocking up the scene to see how it will look. The platelayers' hut, sleepers and ballast bin can be made off the layout on the workbench. They can then be positioned on the bare baseboards to get an idea as to how the finished scene will look. You may prefer the ballast bin to be on the left rather than the right. Also, add some

rolling stock to the track to see how it interacts with the scene that you are developing.

Once you are happy with your composition, all the elements can be permanently affixed to the layout. Any finishing work can be done such as painting the fencing before starting the scenic work. This stage is just as important whether it is a ballast groundcover or grass and weeds since it will blend the individual elements into the layout as a whole. Once the scenic work is completed, small details such as the platelayers' tools can be added to finish off the scene.

Although this scene revolving around a platelayers' hut is a small one, because it is not usually possible to model a lot of lineside in O gauge, there is certainly plenty of modelling that can be done. The completed scene is very interesting to look at when there are no trains passing by. The focus on detail means that many enjoyable hours can be spent building the scene, with an end result that will be rewarding for many years to come.

This lineside scene is in O gauge and will depict a platelayers' hut and various details around it. The starting point is to lay out the key components of the scene to check that they will fit and to try different arrangements until you find the one that you like best.

An overall aerial view of the completed O gauge platelayers' hut scene showing the hut as the central focal point. The piles of sleepers and the ballast bin help to extend the scene beyond just the hut itself. Some of the details like the whistle sign and the gradient sign are not related to the platelayers' hut setting, but there is no reason why they cannot be included without overloading the scene.

This close-up view outside the platelayers' hut shows the high level of detail that can be incorporated into O gauge, in this case the various tools from a Peco detailing kit. The figures are white metal and also from Peco; there are six figures in the pack, but the inclusion of just two of them helps to keep the scene in proportion as using them all would literally crowd the scene.

The highly detailed plaster-cast ballast bin by Ten Commandments does feature a representation of ballast within it; however, it is always best to fill the bin with the actual ballast that you are using on the layout to ensure a perfect match in terms of granularity and colour.

RIGHT: The piles of sleepers are another Ten Commandments plaster-cast product, which, once painted and blended into the overall scene, will add a convincing level of detail. The scratch-built wire-in-post fencing at the rear marks the boundary of the railway's land.

A gradient sign is a relatively small item, though in O gauge there is the chance to model it accurately and convincingly. By mounting it into a hole in the baseboard before completing the ballasting, the sign really looks like it has been planted into the ground. The grinding wheel is part of the Peco detailing kit of platelayers' tools.

An eye-level view down the track shows the whole scene in perspective. The platelayers with their tools provide a detailed scene outside their hut, while other elements around this focal point provide depth to the whole scene. Only a very small area of the lineside is represented, but by using O gauge to achieve high levels of detail, it looks amazingly realistic.

THE MODERN ERA IN AN URBAN SETTING

This scene is a very modern one, again in OO gauge to maximize the possibilities for detailing. Despite its modern setting, there can still be a few throwbacks to an earlier age. There is no single centrepiece that dominates the scene, rather a series of elements. The resulting stretch of lineside is typical in its apparent banality, yet there are numerous fine details that bring it to life and make it as realistic as possible.

The scene is about 1m (3.2ft) long, which is a reasonable length of lineside that could connect, for example, a station to a fiddle yard at one end of a layout. The setting is urban, the main giveaway being the high retaining walls at the rear of the layout. While not exclusively an urban feature, the presence of a burnt-out car and the results of fly-tipping suggest a built-up area rather than a countryside setting.

It is a good idea to try various ways of setting out the elements in the available space in order to see what works and what does not. Some are givens, such as the retaining wall being at the rear while the fencing is at the front, though the latter does offer some variation, since there are different configurations possible with the fencing, not least the location of the gates.

The infrastructure of the modern railway is an essential feature in order to help place the scene in the context of the modern era. Features such as relay cabinets, concrete trunking, colour light signals and track workers dressed in high-visibility safety clothing all help to give a modern feel. Having said that, some steam era infrastructure does still survive, the most common being the signal box, many of which lie abandoned but some of which are, for the time being, still in daily use.

The various elements used in this scene also demonstrate that it is always a good idea to cast around for products that can be used. You can research what is available by reference to catalogues, magazine adverts and manufacturer websites. The various products used in the scene have been supplied by a total of twelve different manufacturers. The popularity of OO gauge means that it is well supported by a wide number of manufacturers, both large and small.

As always, it is advisable to lay out the elements of the lineside scene in various different configurations in order to see which one works best or is the most pleasing. Elements such as the high retaining wall are a given, but the position of others such as the signals, relay cabinets and signal box offer a near infinite number of possibilities.

This overall view of the completed scene shows some differences in the position of certain elements from the initial mock-up. The foreground features mostly modern railway infrastructure, such as relay cabinets and concrete trunking looking well maintained and efficient; however, the 'other side of the tracks' is more run-down, with a vandalized disused signal box, fly-tipping and a burnt-out car.

A feature of modern track maintenance is that the permanent-way gang now arrives in the ubiquitous white van (by Oxford Diecast) and there are fewer people involved. If you want to put a van at the lineside, remember to include some way for it to drive there rather than just materializing out of nowhere. This view shows the wide double gates in the security fencing for vehicular access. Note that just a few figures (by Bachmann Scenecraft) have been used, as would be correct for general maintenance and inspection (unlike full track renewal).

Sometimes, the maintenance vans park outside the security fencing and all that is needed is a small personnel gate for access. This part of the scene shows just such a gate, which is used for access to the small relay cabinet (by Wills) adjacent to the concrete cable trunking. One solitary worker (from the Bachmann Scenecraft range) in a high-visibility vest is checking the track fixings on the sleepers. Note that he is standing safely out of the way of passing trains.

Modern security fencing is of the palisade type, made from metal panels topped with various degrees of spikes securely bolted to metal posts. This model fencing is by Knightwing International. Note the empty cable drums on the railway side of the fence. These are actually N-gauge items from York Modelmaking, but it is a fine example of how some products can be successfully used in either a larger or smaller scale than the one for which they were intended.

Most modern railway locations are now fully signalled by colour lights (although semaphore signals can still be found for a while yet). This is a non-working three-aspect colour light signal with a feather for a junction as produced by Model Scene Accessories. The concrete cable trunking seen right and centre is by Wills, which leads into scratch-built trunking on the left made from rectangular plastic strip. The single figure (by Bachmann Scenecraft) is checking for oncoming trains before climbing the signal ladder to perform maintenance.

This elevated view shows the Wills cable trunking to advantage, especially the T-section junction pieces that lead to relay cabinets (also by Wills). The cabinets are standing on a simple concrete foundation made from a piece of card the same height as the trunking. The signal and relay cabinet on the other side of the tracks are produced by Model Scene Accessories and the two sides are linked by a plastic pipe for the cables that was simply made from a piece of orange-coloured electrical wire.

Unfortunately, rubbish often accumulates at the lineside, despite the obvious safety implications. The washing machines, cookers, sofa, mattress and carpet were produced from a Scalescenes downloadable PDF. Not all lineside rubbish is the result of fly-tippers. The empty cable drum (by York Modelmaking) has been left by track workers, while the pile of bricks (by Harburn Hobbies) is all that remains of a demolished platelayers' hut.

There is no need to use the same type of boundary protection exclusively throughout an entire layout; in real life, things change as required. On the right is a high brick wall (scratch-built from card covered with brick paper). This has been damaged in the centre and so patched up with some wooden slatted fencing (by Ratio Plastic Models). The wall has gone completely on the left, so it has been replaced by palisade fencing (by Knightwing International).

WATER TROUGHS IN A REMOTE COUNTRY SCENE

Most of the railway network consists of largely featureless railway line in the middle of nowhere as the job of the railway is to link places. The railway in the countryside is rarely modelled, since it requires quite a lot of space to portray convincingly the countryside through which the railway passes. There is also a tendency to want to include a station, which means some amount of habitation and at the very least a road.

Since a fair amount of room is required to portray the open space of the countryside, the smallest commercial scale is ideal. Therefore, N gauge has been used to create this scene. The classic features of the steam era lineside are included, namely wooden fencing and telegraph poles. You could just stop at this and would have an utterly realistic lineside scene. A platelayers' hut is included, as these were placed quite regularly.

In order to make the scene a little more interesting and unique, water troughs have been included, along with the signs to indicate the point where the troughs start. In order to supply the water troughs and keep them topped up quickly, there is a large water tower incorporated into the scene. Otherwise, this scene simply portrays the idea of a thin railway line cutting through green and pleasant lands.

For contrast and to illustrate different products, two types of lineside fencing have been used, one on each side of the track. In reality, the same fencing would be used consistently unless, say, one side had needed to be heavily repaired or even replaced.

This bird's-eye view of the whole countryside scene modelled in N gauge shows how the railway line cuts through the open expanse of fields. The water tower to supply the water troughs provides something a little out of the ordinary; if it were not included, the bland scene of track, fencing and telegraph poles would be perfectly representative of the steam era for most of the railway lines in Britain.

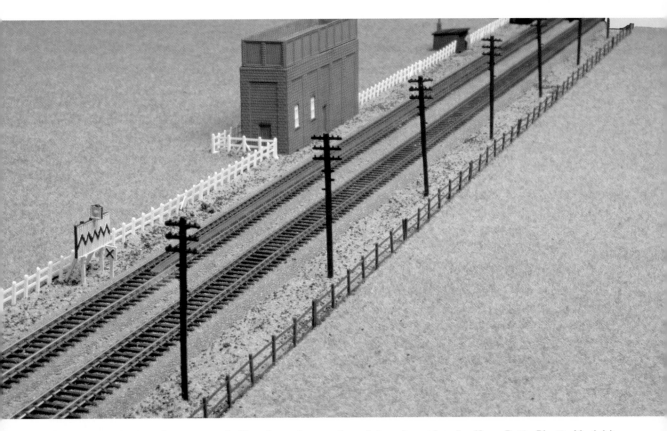

An acute-angle view shows to good effect the regimentation of the telegraph poles (from Ratio Plastic Models). The signs on the left indicate the start of the water trough (also by Ratio Plastic Models), which can itself be seen on the left-hand track.

The flat-roofed wooden platelayers' hut is from a Peco kit and the solitary figure is also from the same company. Although a track gang could be modelled beside the line, the reality is more likely to be a complete absence of people on a remote stretch of lineside.

The telegraph poles and foreground fencing are from kits by Ratio Plastic Models, while the white fencing at the rear is manufactured by Kestrel Designs. The latter also makes the kit for the water tower, which in this case is two kits joined into one in order to create a more imposing structure.

There is not much more that can be said about a scene like this, since it is a case of 'less is more'. The water troughs are, perhaps, an indulgence, although they were often found in the middle of nowhere as that could be the point where steam locomotives needed to replenish their water supply without the inconvenience of having to stop.

THE STEAM ERA LINESIDE IN THE COUNTRYSIDE

There are many features of railway infrastructure that modellers often include in a layout depicting a station scene. Examples of such features include signal boxes, level crossings and signals. Yet there is no reason why many of these features cannot be incorporated into a scene that depicts the railway line outside of the environs of the station.

This OO gauge scene depicts the most popular era for railway modellers, namely the post-nationalization steam era. This was a time before modernization

swept away many of the traditional elements of the lineside, such as semaphore signals and gated level crossings, to replace them with features that have now become familiar, such as colour light signals, concrete trunking and relay cabinets.

The setting is very much a countryside one with open fields on either side of the railway, although it would be easy to change this to an urban scene if required by replacing the fields with houses and factories. The boundary fencing might well be replaced with brick walls, but every one of the other elements would be just as appropriate.

Quite a lot of elements have been incorporated into a scene that is just 1m (3.2ft) long, but without overpowering the scene or making it look cluttered. If this is the only amount of space available on a layout, say between a station and a fiddle yard, it allows the modeller the chance to represent the railway 'in the middle of nowhere'. If a greater length of baseboard is available, the scene could be stretched out; for example, the platelayers' hut could be positioned

This aerial view of the complete scene shows how much detail can be incorporated into a short stretch of lineside without overcrowding it or making it look unrealistic. The elements are a mix of ready-made items and kits that are easy to assemble and finish. It provides a perfect setting for any region and train to pass through.

further away. The level crossing could be moved further away as well, although it might preferably be kept within sight of the signal box so that the signalman could operate the gates. If you did move the level crossing, it gives the opportunity to have a crossing keeper's cottage so that the crossing is independent of the signal box.

The inclusion of a track gang hard at work makes for a nice cameo scene, but the challenge is always to include the figures without them interfering with the passage of trains. This problem has been overcome for this scene by having the track gang work on a completely isolated piece of track. The period of nationalization was also the start of rationalization, so it is assumed that the track gang are in the process of removing a disconnected siding or part of a disused junction to a now closed branch line.

Despite being a scene in 'the middle of nowhere', there are quite a lot of people in the scene. The track gang numbers thirteen figures, reflecting the very manual and labour-intensive nature of the pre-modernization railway. The solitary fogman outside his hut makes a nice cameo in his own right. Finally, there is the group of four schoolboys with their notebooks and Ian Allan 'ABCs', eagerly awaiting the next train in case it is a rare locomotive. Perhaps one of those schoolboys has now grown up to become a railway modeller, building an accurate piece of railway lineside in order to take him back to the happy memories of his youth.

Looking down the single-track line reveals a number of different cameo scenes such as the fogman and the track gang, which collectively do not overcrowd the overall scene. Any one of the scenes could be used without the others on the principle that 'less is more', or they could be distributed around a larger layout if plenty of room is available for a bigger model railway layout.

The focal point of the scene is this signal box (built from a Wills kit). As a two-storey building, it gives some height to the scene, as does the distant signal, which is a ready-to-plant item from Hornby. The telegraph poles are also a Hornby product; note how their bases (glued to the baseboard) have been hidden by carefully applying ballast around them.

The sturdy brick-built platelayers' hut (from a Ratio Plastic Models kit) provides sound accommodation for the track workers, one of whom is acting as lookout for the track gang. The milepost and gradient signs are easily scratch-built, although these are Hornby ready-made products; their substantial plastic bases have been hidden under a layer of ballast. The wooden fencing in the foreground is from a Ratio Plastic Models kit.

The level crossing is made from a Dapol kit, the base of which has been cut down slightly to match the level of track glued directly to the baseboard. The stone walling that protects both the railway line and the lane beyond is a ready-made product from Hornby, which could be repainted if a particular local stone needed to be represented. Hornby also provides the whistle sign, which once again has a substantial plastic base covered by ballast.

With careful construction and painting, the Dapol level crossing kit can be made so that the gates can be moved by hand. Most level crossing kits in all the modelling scales can be made so that the gates or barriers can be moved, allowing a scene to be set up for a photograph such as this. The GPO van is a ready-made Oxford Diecast product.

The plastic figures in the track gang from Dapol are easily painted and once suitably posed on the layout, they look very authentic. Note the logical grouping of figures, for example the three men at the back are using poles to lever up a piece of rail. A couple of short lengths of rusty rail form part of the lineside 'rubbish' often left behind after maintenance work.

The fogman must have seen the weather forecast, as he is wrapped up in a thick overcoat and scarf and his brazier is well stoked. With his hut, he is positioned near a signal, since his job in actual fog would be to provide additional signalling, possibly even putting detonators on the line. These items are from Model Scene Accessories, while the larger Ten Commandments fogman's hut at the rear is in this case serving as the outside toilet for the adjacent signal box. The same company also makes the sleeper-built fencing at the rear.

These exquisitely produced schoolboy figures are available from Bachmann Scenecraft and they look perfect stood by the lineside waiting for their next 'cop'. For many modellers, this small cameo will take them back to their own schoolboy trainspotting days and have them reaching for their well-thumbed Ian Allan 'ABC'. You really can travel back in time when you model the lineside.

USEFUL CONTACTS

Aidan Campbell Miniatures
22 Queens Road, Hoylake, Wirral CH47 2AH
www.aidan-campbell.co.uk
Manufacturer of model railway figures.

Ancorton Models
www.ancortonmodels.com
Manufacturer of scenic accessories in N gauge.

Bachmann Scenecraft
Bachmann Ltd, Moat Way, Barwell, Leicestershire
    LE9 8EY
www.bachmann.co.uk
Manufacturer of ready-made scenic accessories,
    buildings and figures.

Corgi
Hornby Hobbies Ltd
Westwood, Margate, Kent, CT9 4JX
Tel: 01843 233525
www.corgi.co.uk
Manufacturer of road vehicles.

Dapol
Gledrid Industrial Park, Chirk,
    Wrexham LL14 5DG
Tel: 01691 774455
www.dapol.co.uk
Manufacturer of plastic scenic accessory kits.

Dornaplas
2 Springside Cottages, Dornafield Road, Ipplepen,
    Newton Abbot, Devon TQ12 5SJ
Tel: 01803 813749
www.springsidemodels.com
Manufacturer of plastic kits for buildings and road
    vehicles.

Evergreen Scale Models
65 Bradrock Dr, DesPlaines, Illinois 60018, USA
www.evergreenscalemodels.com
Supplier of plastic model parts.

Fleetline Road 'n' Rail
Lytchett Manor Models, 48 Woolavington Road,
    Puriton, Bridgwater, Somerset TA7 8BQ
Tel: 01278 685302
www.lytchettmanor.co.uk
Manufacturer of white-metal kits, scenic accessories
    and details.

Gaugemaster Controls Ltd
Gaugemaster House, Ford Road, Arundel, West
    Sussex BN18 0BN
Tel: 01903 884488
www.gaugemaster.com
Manufacturer of controllers and scenic accessories,
    as well as a shop with a comprehensive selection
    of models.

Harburn Hobbies
67 Elm Row, Leith Walk, Edinburgh EH7 4AQ
Tel: 0131 556 3233
www.harburnhobbies.co.uk
Supplier of scenic accessories.

Hornby Hobbies Ltd
Westwood, Margate, Kent, CT9 4JX
Tel: 01843 233525
www.hornby.com
Manufacturer of Skaledale and Lydle End resin-cast
    scenic accessories.

Kestrel Designs
Gaugemaster House, Ford Road, Arundel, West
    Sussex BN18 0BN

Tel: 01903 884488
www.gaugemaster.com
Versatile range of plastic kits for buildings supplied
by Gaugemaster.

Knightwing International
Malham Works, 33 Almondbury Bank, Huddersfield,
West Yorkshire HD5 8HE
Tel: 01484 537191
www.knightwing.co.uk
Manufacturer of plastic and white-metal kits.

Langley Models
166 Three Bridges Road, Crawley, Sussex RH10 1LE
Tel: 01293 516329
www.langleymodels.co.uk
Manufacturer of white-metal kits, scenic accessories
and details.

Metcalfe Models & Toys
Bell Busk, Skipton BD23 4DU
Tel: 01729 830072
Manufacturer of die-cut card kits for buildings.

Model Scene Accessories
Pritchard Patent Product Co. Ltd, Beer, Devon
EX12 3NA
Tel: 01297 21542
www.peco-uk.com
Manufacturer of scenic accessories.

Model Signal Engineering
PO Box 70, Barton upon Humber DN18 5XY
Tel: 01652 635885
www.modelsignals.com
Manufacturer of semaphore signalling parts for
model railways.

Oxford Diecast
Tel: 02380 248850
www.oxforddiecast.co.uk
Manufacturer of die-cast road vehicles, including
cars, buses, coaches and lorries.

P&D Marsh
The Stables, Wakes End Farm, Eversholt, Milton
Keynes, Buckinghamshire MK17 9FB
Tel: 01525 280068
www.pdmarshmodels.com
Manufacturer of white-metal kits, scenic accessories
and details.

Peco
Peco Technical Advice Bureau, Underleys, Beer,
Devon EX12 3NA
Tel: 01297 21542
www.peco-uk.com
Manufacturer of track, wagons, kits for buildings and
scenic accessories.

Plastruct
www.plastruct.com
Supplier of plastic model parts.

Preiser
www.preiserfiguren.de
Manufacturer of figures and accessories.

Ratio Plastic Models
Ratio House, Mardle Way, Buckfastleigh, Devon
TQ11 0NR
Tel: 01364 642764
www.peco-uk.com
Manufacturer of plastic kits for buildings and signals.

Roxey Mouldings
58 Dudley Road, Walton-on-Thames, Surrey
KT12 2JU
Tel: 01932 245439
www.roxeymouldings.co.uk

Scalescenes
www.scalescenes.com
Manufacturer of downloadable PDF files for card
kits, papers and accessories.

Slater's Plastikard

Old Road, Darley Dale, Matlock, Derbyshire
  DE4 2ER
Tel: 01629 73405
www.slatersplastikard.com
Manufacturer of embossed plastic sheets of walling
  materials.

Smart Models

www.smartmodels.co.uk
Manufacturer of downloadable PDF files for card
  kits, papers and accessories.

Superquick Model Kits

The Red House, Axminster, Devon EX13 5SE
Tel: 01297 631435
www.superquick.co.uk
Manufacturer of card model building kits for OO
  gauge.

Ten Commandments

20 Struan Drive, Inverkeithing, Fife KY11 1AR
Tel: 01383 410032
www.cast-in-stone.co.uk
Manufacturer of details, wagon loads and low-relief
  buildings cast in plaster.

Wills

Pritchard Patent Product Co. Ltd, Beer, Devon
  EX12 3NA
Tel: 01297 21542
www.peco-uk.com
Manufacturer of kits for buildings and lineside
  accessories.

York Modelmaking and Display Ltd

Unit 13, The Bull Commercial Centre,
  Stockton-on-the-Forest, York YO32 9LE
Tel: 01904 400358
www.yorkmodelmaking.com
Supplier of laser-cut plastic accessories for all the
  major scales.

INDEX

RELATED TITLES FROM CROWOOD

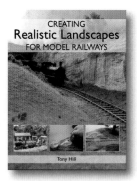

CREATING REALISTIC LANDSCAPES FOR MODEL RAILWAYS

TONY HILL

ISBN 978 1 84797 219 4

160pp, 395 illustrations

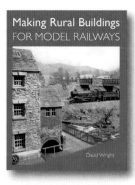

MAKING RURAL BUILDINGS FOR MODEL RAILWAYS

DAVID WRIGHT

ISBN 978 1 84797 460 0

192pp, 320 illustrations

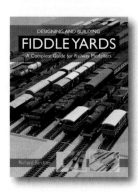

DESIGNING AND BUILDING FIDDLE YARDS

RICHARD BARDSLEY

ISBN 978 1 84797 816 5

176pp, 140 illustrations

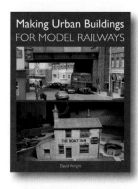

MAKING URBAN BUILDINGS FOR MODEL RAILWAYS

DAVID WRIGHT

ISBN 978 1 84797 568 3

192pp, 340 illustrations

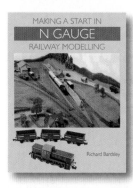

MAKING A START IN N GAUGE RAILWAY MODELLING

RICHARD BARDSLEY

ISBN 978 1 84797 556 0

192pp, 300 illustrations

PLANNING, DESIGNING AND MAKING RAILWAY LAYOUTS IN SMALL SPACES

RICHARD BARDSLEY

ISBN 978 1 84797 424 2

144pp, 130 illustrations

In case of difficulty ordering, please contact the Sales Office:

The Crowood Press
Ramsbury
Wiltshire
SN8 2HR
UK

Tel: 44 (0) 1672 520320

enquiries@crowood.com

www.crowood.com